Patanjali in the Light

A New Paradigm for Understanding the Yoga Sutras

No part of this book is to be taken as a substitute for psychological counseling, therapy or medical advice. Please consult your healthcare provider or therapist before making or implementing any changes based on this book.

Copyright © 2018, Paul Dugliss. All rights reserved. No part of this book may be reproduced by any means without the written permission of the publisher.

Cover Design: Paul Dugliss

Contents

1. Patanjali in the Light (Introduction)
   a. Patanjali in the Light 11
   b. The Higher States of Consciousness 24
   c. The First Key — The Four Quarters 33
   d. The Second Key — Meditation 37
   e. The Third Key — Concentration Versus Concentrated ... 39
   f. The Fourth Key — The Monk Versus the Householder ... 41
2. First Quarter — Samadhi (Pure Consciousness)
   a. The Process of Transcending - Key to the First Quarter ... 47
   b. The Second Key to the First Quarter — the Field of Consciousness 50
   c. The First Quarter Translated 54
3. Second Quarter — Sadhana (Establishing Perpetual Consciousness / Cosmic Consciousness)
   a. The Key to the Second Quarter — The End and the Means 73
   b. Second Quarter Translated 79

4. Third Quarter — Vibhuti (Bliss Consciousness)
    a. Key One to the Third Quarter — Love and Bliss 105
    b. Key Two: How Creation Manifests 109
    c. Third Quarter Translated 117
5. Fourth Quarter — Kaivalya (Unity Consciousness)
    a. The Key to the Fourth Quarter: Dissolving
       Latent Impressions 129
    b. Fourth Quarter Translated 132
6. Making It Practical — The Last Key 139
7. Resources 143

*Dedicated to
seekers everywhere*

Acknowledgements

With all gratitude to my many teachers, especially Charlie Lutes, David McClanahan, Maharishi Mahesh Yogi, my father Malcolm Graham Dugliss, Maharishi Sahasiva Isham, and the many others who have guided and taught me. Special acknowledgement to my wife for her loving support of my many endeavors.

Patanjali in the Light

It is a great pleasure to present this knowledge of yoga brought into the light. What a wondrous gift the sage Patanjali has offered us — a gift of great wisdom and insight. This amazing insight is not just an explanation of yoga; rather, it is a deep insight into the functioning of the human being and the vast potential we hold.

Within each of us is a great potential for liberation, higher consciousness and freedom from suffering. What a glorious time we live in, when we can view the ancient wisdom in the light of modern science and come to the most profound understanding of what life offers us.

To bring Patanjali's Yoga *Sutras* into the brightest light and allow it to shine in its full glory, we must first understand how consciousness works, how the human mind works and how yoga, or union, is actually attained. We must learn a bit about human neurophysiology and how it works to support and promote higher states of consciousness.

Patanjali's Yoga *Sutras* are ancient wisdom. Like every form of wisdom that has been passed down, codified or written down in an ancient language, clear interpretation is paramount. It depends on deep understanding. It depends on becoming familiar with the context in which the wisdom was originally offered. And frequently the wisdom is encoded in language and metaphor. Understanding this code requires certain keys. It is my joy to present those keys to you.

It is time that the inner workings of yoga be known and taught, understood and utilized. It is time that the truth be made clear, plain and straightforward. This is knowledge that transforms lives. It is so widely needed, and it is now available through the great blessings of a modern science that gives a framework for all the many interpretations of Patanjali to be unified.

Patanjali gives us two very important gifts. The first is a profound knowledge of accelerated inner growth — growth that is mystical and spiritual and yet grounded in our ability to more deeply perceive reality. It enables us to know and to be aware and awake in every aspect and facet of life.

The second is the great gift of an end to suffering — a map of the territory of full human development. It provides inspiration for us to come out of the painful, intense, and often discouraging elements of human existence and enter into the light. It is not a matter of intellectual discourse — it is a matter of us utilizing this knowledge and applying it in a practical manner to our daily lives.

This deepest understanding resonates in our hearts. We know what it is like to suffer, and here is one who has come out of the suffering. Patanjali offers us a map to a new and transformed life. This is the gift of the enlightened — Patanjali's gift. From the very first sentence, the very first *sutra*, the very first words, the profundity of this exposition is so deep that it simply resonates and echoes in the heart: *Atha Yoga* — Now yoga! When the mind views these words, all sorts of interpretations come forth. But when viewed from the heart, they convey the heart's longing for freedom and liberation and the relief that it is finally realized: "At last! And now we have come there: Now yoga will be explained."

We can receive and understand his gift when we listen with the heart and have the proper keys to unlock it. One such key is understanding that when the enlightened offer such gifts, they speak from their level of spiritual development. They speak at the level they have attained. They speak from their reality. They speak from what is clear to them. Likewise, the student listens from

A New Paradigm

his or her level of reality — from his or her level of wakefulness and from a limited level of concept and experience. This gap is responsible for much of this wonderful knowledge of evolution being almost completely lost. It is the blessing of this time that we have found ways to overcome this gap and find the true wisdom of yoga.

Patanjali's Yoga *Sutras* are not an intellectual discourse. They are the teaching of an enlightened sage instructing his disciples on the nature of consciousness and evolution, so that they may evolve quickly. Its purpose is to create within us a state of liberation, a state of enlightenment. But you can't get somewhere if you don't know where you are going, and you can't understand a foreign map without the proper keys to its symbols. Thus it is with Patanjali. And as much as Patanjali gives us a map, he doesn't build an airplane for us to get there quickly. His *Sutras* give us the overview, not the specific means.

> *Patanjali is the master teacher who, in a matter of a few sentences, gives us the picture, the map and the description of all of life and the mechanics of how it works.*

Patanjali in the Light

Understand that the great sages were so used to their state of evolvement that they frequently had difficulty describing the details; thus, the process and the mechanics of how it works have not always been clearly communicated.

Patanjali, on the other hand, is brilliant in describing all of life and all of the workings of consciousness — the dynamics of inner life and the road to liberation and enlightenment — and he does so in less than two hundred sentences. That is simply amazing. Patanjali is the master teacher who, in a matter of a few sentences, gives us the picture, the map and the description of all of life and the mechanics of how it works.

In order to understand that map — that broad view and its implications for our inner growth and development — five keys are necessary:

1. An understanding of the context of Patanajali's daily experience and what he simply assumed we would comprehend.
2. An understanding of the seven states of consciousness and the four higher states of consciousness.
3. An understanding of how the human brain works.
4. A grasp of how enlightened knowledge is reclaimed:
    a. An understanding of the difference between the monk's path and the householder's path.

    b. An understanding of the end versus the means.
    c. An understanding of intellectual versus experiential knowledge.
    d. An understanding of the map versus territory.
5. Knowing the key to the structure of the *Sutras* — The Four Quarters and what they mean.

What Patanjali Assumed

With a context for understanding the level of human growth and evolution attained by Patanjali, it is easy to see what he may have taken for granted. His students were likely very advanced, and therefore he could skip a lot of details. Without context, it is like someone handing you a map and pointing to what looks like a river here and some mountains there. You would be confused if you didn't have the context of the map or the place it represented. Suppose the location is Russia. Without that context, you would be lost with or without the map. And so it is with the Yoga *Sutras*. Patanjali gives us a map of life. He gives us precious wisdom, and with the proper keys and a proper understanding of human evolution and inner growth, we can discover how amazing his exposition is.

What is needed, and what we will start with, is an explanation of how human growth works. With this we can understand the level from which Patanjali speaks. By understanding this higher level of consciousness, his very concise set of sayings gives us an exquisite map of inner growth and development.

The best way for us to understand the relationship between Patanjali's map and our inner experience is through an analogy of how the nervous system develops in childhood. It is through our nervous system that we interact with and understand our day-to-day reality.

This analogy comes from developmental psychology. Jean Piaget revolutionized developmental psychology. Only two theories of development were widely accepted before his work gained acceptance. One was the Freudian theory — different stages of development based on animalistic impulses and how the human being learns to mitigate and negotiate those. The other contrasting theory was behaviorism — that the growth of a child was completely based on Pavlovian association and reinforcement of behavior. These were the two major theories of how children grow and personality develops.

Rather than doing large-scale studies with children, Piaget understood human development and the nervous system's role in it through making very careful observations, starting with

A New Paradigm

his own children. Piaget's genius was that he realized that children are not simply inexperienced and uneducated — they fundamentally think differently. And these differences are based on the development of connections within the human brain. He came to realize through his observations that children's nervous systems caused them *to experience reality differently,* depending on the stage of growth they were in.

Up until his time, it was assumed that children were simply less experienced, not as educated, not as astute or logical as adults. To remedy this, educators simply attempted to pour more information into children. Piaget demonstrated that that view was totally wrong. Children actually think differently, perceive reality differently, and need something more than experience, learning or training. They need growth and development of the connections within their brains.

The best demonstration of this comes at age four or five for most children. Take a tall glass cylinder and a wide bowl and a pitcher of water. First, fill the pitcher to the top and pour the water into the cylinder. Then fill the pitcher again, and pour its contents into the bowl. Then ask the child which container holds more. Invariably, the child will choose one or the other — they will not say that they hold the same. This is because the child's brain is wired to think in only one dimension. It is not two-dimensional.

PATANJALI IN THE LIGHT

Take a cylinder, a bowl and 1-cup measuring cup.

In front of a four-year-old, fill the cup with water and pour into the cylinder. Fill again and pour into the bowl.

Ask the four-year-old, "Which has more, the cylinder or the bowl?"

GUESS WHAT THEY WILL SAY???

A New Paradigm

If the child focuses on the height dimension, he or she will say the cylinder holds much more water than the bowl because it is so much higher. That is the reasoning; that expresses what is real for the child. If the child focuses instead on the width and sees that the bowl is much wider, the only logical conclusion is that it must hold more water than the thin column. It does not matter how many times you pour the water from the same pitcher. It does not matter how much logic you use or how you try to teach this. It does not matter if you give the child candy to reinforce the right answer. If you do reward them for saying the amounts are the same, and they agree that they are the same, and then you pull them aside after the experiment and ask them if they really believe they are the same, they will say, "No, I just wanted the candy — they really are different."

Now imagine if the development of the human nervous system stopped at this point. We would be left with two camps of people — those who focus mainly on the vertical dimension and those who focus on the horizontal dimension. This inability to perceive reality in its entirety would make for many conflicts. We can imagine different political parties or religions evolving, each one believing it is right and the other wrong and never realizing that neither is seeing the full picture.

Imagine further in this religious and political climate that someone found a way to stunt everyone's nervous system at the status of an eight-year-old's. Imagine then that a person comes out of the mountains and starts talking about how the cylinder and the bowl really hold the same amount of water. To the very "practical" and "grounded" verticalists and horizontalists, this is just mystical mumbo jumbo. All this talk of things being the same and talk of unity is simply seen as not real. What our mystic from the mountains knows to be reality is outside what the average person can conceive of *because the nervous system of the average person is not developed.*

Patanjali is that mystic sage from the mountain. What he sees as reality is far beyond what we perceive *because we have yet to develop our nervous systems.* Thus, Patanjali's gift remains unreceived by far too many.

What did Patanjali assume from his high state of consciousness? At his level, the human energy system is completely obvious. This is why Patanjali does not go through a description of the chakras and the energy system. Just as when a yoga teacher describes a yoga posture, there is no need to say to the student, "You have two shoulders. They are symmetrical and on each side of the body, above your elbows." For Patanjali, knowledge of the human subtle energy system and the chakras was assumed.

A New Paradigm

You will also not find Patanjali speaking about love. His whole exposition is an offering of love. It is his love for his students and humanity that inspires the entire discourse. It is out of love that he shows us a map of our human potential. Why would he need to speak of love, when one lives in an ocean of love in higher consciousness? It is simply assumed. Love is the essence of the being of the sage. In his high state, having established himself in *Sat Chit Ananada* (Absolute bliss consciousness), the bliss and joy and love that are inherent in being radiate forth in each moment, in each expression, in each word. The whole exposition is an expression of love and divinity. The closest he comes to speaking of love is in using the word "devotion."

Patanjali's whole exposition is an offering of love. It is his love for his students and humanity that inspires the entire discourse.

Likewise, Patanjali gives little mention of Divinity or God or the Universe. The holiness and respect for life is inherent in the expressions of Patanjali. The respect for the inherent nature of the universe and the preciousness of human potential is not discussed, rather it is demonstrated.

Even the postures of yoga are only referenced in three of the almost two hundred *Sutras*. Again, it was taken for granted that we had a grasp of the relationship of consciousness, mind and body.

Just like the eight-year-olds' world in the above analogy, Patanjali's world is baffling to us. His expressions are confusing because we don't share the experience of higher consciousness. Our nervous systems have not yet embraced our ability to perceive reality fully. This, then is the key: *The ability to perceive the truth, to know reality, is dependent upon the growth of the connections within the human brain.*

While we may not have the ability to perceive at his level, we can intellectually get a feel for the context of his greatness by understanding how consciousness develops. An intellectual understanding of the higher states of consciousness will allow us to understand the profundity of his gift to humanity. More important, we cannot understand his work without having this foundation. Ultimately, Patanjali speaks about higher states of consciousness and the vast potential we hold within us. Of necessity then, before we can dive into the *Sutras* themselves, we must gain a deeper understanding of consciousness. While this creates a very long introduction, it will be worth it. It will allow us to fully appreciate the wisdom and wonder of Patanjali.

The Higher States of Consciousness

In order to comprehend the *Sutras* of Patanjali, we need to understand the four higher states of consciousness. The first of these states is key to the other states of consciousness — they are built from repeatedly experiencing and integrating this first higher state of consciousness. To understand the higher states of consciousness, let us look at the ones we are familiar with already:

1. Deep Sleep
2. Dream Sleep
3. Waking State

Each state has its hallmark, its relationship to the external environment, its internal experience, and finally, its characteristic brainwave patterns.

For the state we call Deep Sleep, we have no awareness of the environment, we have no awareness of ourselves, and we have a predominance of delta waves on the EEG (electroencephalogram — used for recording and analyzing brainwaves). The hallmark of this state of consciousness is the complete absence of awareness.

The next state of consciousness is Dream Sleep. This state is characterized by no awareness of the external environment and a vague and distorted sense of ourselves in dreams. The EEG will often show large discharges of electrical energy (in Rapid Eye Movement sleep or REM sleep, where most dreaming takes place). The hallmark of this state of consciousness is unreliable impressions — the dream experience is not a reliable representation of reality.

The third commonly experienced state of consciousness is the Waking State. This state is characterized by an overwhelming awareness of the external environment and our thoughts about it and our reactions to it, emotional and otherwise. In this state, thinking, feeling and sensing tend to overwhelm our awareness, resulting in little awareness of our own consciousness. We lose who it is who is sensing, thinking and feeling. In that sense, the mystics often refer to the waking state as the "waking dream." We are awake to the environment, but our thoughts, feelings and senses overshadow ourselves so much, it becomes as if we are lost in a dream. The hallmark of this state of consciousness is awareness of the environment and our reactions to it. The EEG brainwaves show a predominance of beta waves that are usually not synchronized (not coherent across different areas of the brain).

Given the familiar states of consciousness as reference points, we can now discuss the higher states of consciousness. The first higher state of consciousness comes when we turn our attention inward and go beyond thought, beyond sensation, beyond emotion and feeling, and we experience our Pure Self — that self that witnesses all of the rest of our life. It is hard to describe this state without directly experiencing it. Of interest, though, is that in order to fall asleep, we must undergo this process of turning inward away from external input from the senses and away from thought. We must turn our awareness away from the environment and our thoughts and feelings. In this transition most of us enter into sleep. However, in meditation, we remain in a relaxed state of wakefulness. We are wide awake and completely aware, but that awareness is without any content.

This state of consciousness appears to be characterized by coherent alpha waves in the frontal lobes of the brain. It is also characterized by obliviousness to the environment. Low-level stimuli like shuffling feet in the room are not perceived. The individual's awareness is fully turned inward beyond thought, sensation and feeling to a level of pure awareness. This fourth state of consciousness is sometimes called Transcendental Consciousness or the state of Pure Consciousness. It is called *Samadhi* in the Yoga and Vedic traditions. It is called *Nirvana* in the Buddhist tradition. It is the window into the *No Mind* of Zen. It is a basic function of the human nervous system. We are all capable of attaining it. It is not some interesting anomaly — it is a basic function.

For us to appreciate this capability of the nervous system, we need to understand a little about the human brain and its function.

How the Brain Works

Different functions are located in different halves of the brain. While what follows is a simplified model of brain structure and function, it serves well to help understand the development of consciousness without going into excruciating detail.

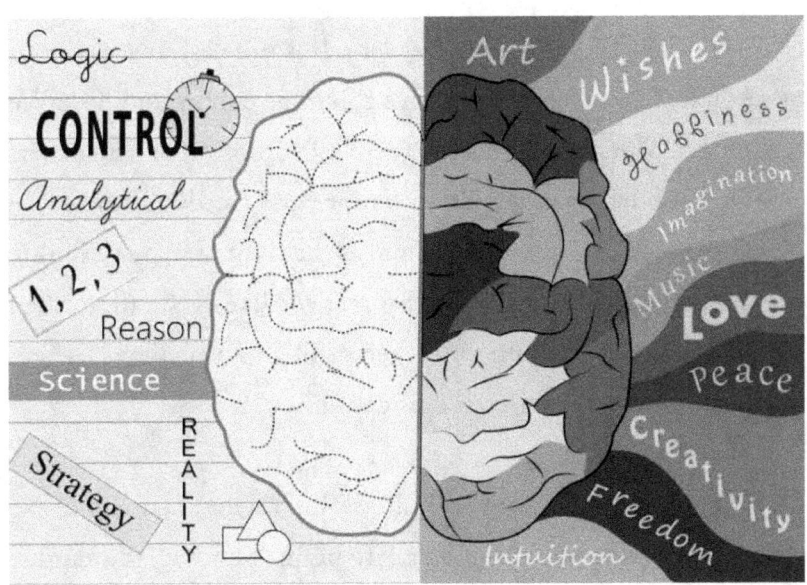

The two hemispheres typically play different roles, and if we want to understand higher consciousness, we need an understanding of both the right and left hemispheres of the brain.

A New Paradigm

The left brain is where we experience the sequential unfolding of time. The left brain is aware of the passage of time — past, present and future. It is where language resides. The ability to analyze and to put together concepts, to use logic to analyze the past and to try to control the future all reside here. As such, much of the programming and patterns of the ego that are language-based are located in the left brain. The ego's attempt to strategize and get needs met is mainly a left-brain activity. Our concept of reality is left-brain as well — again because it is mainly language bound.

In contrast, the right brain is silent. It is timeless. It sees things as a whole. It is where we perceive things as energy and flow. We see patterns of energy and a broader, holistic vision of things. The right brain is where we experience peace and freedom. And as we become more familiar with this, and as the right brain functioning becomes more coherent through practices like meditation, then this peace begins to take on other right-brain qualities — joy, happiness, love or what the yogis call "bliss."

A neuroscientist named Jill Bolte-Taylor had a stroke that temporarily wiped out her left brain. She had the unique situation as a neuroscientist to experience directly brain research that had disclosed functioning of the right brain. She found such peacefulness and amazing continuity of wholeness that she had no sense of anything being wrong. Everything was patterns of energy and bliss and timelessness. Most of us have had this experience of timelessness and blissful joy when falling in love. Romantic love is perceived in the right brain, predominantly, and it contributes to the timeless joy of that experience. Remember the right brain is silent, except for the processing of music. Music and the arts can bring us into that same timeless peace, bliss and joy.

The most direct way to experience the fourth state of consciousness (Pure Consciousness — the first of the higher states of consciousness) is through meditation. In meditation we let go of the left brain's language, reason, control, analysis, logic, concepts of reality and beliefs, and we come to the silence and peace of the right brain. With our eyes closed, the visual cortex gets a break. As we turn deeper inward away from the senses, the frontal lobes become more active and produce coherent alpha waves. We let go of sensation, and we experience wakefulness without thoughts or any content of awareness. We experience just being — pure being.

Understanding this state of consciousness is key, because it is the foundation of all the other higher states of consciousness. As we become more and more familiar with this state of Pure Consciousness, the frontal alpha wave coherency starts to extend into our daily activity. It remains, even though our eyes are open and we are processing input from the environment. The silence and peace of the right brain begin to integrate with the left brain functioning. We are more aware of the gaps between thoughts. We perceive the impressions of the environment without overshadowing the peace and silence of our innermost self. We often have the sense of just witnessing experience, as if the environment and our thoughts about it were merely a movie projected onto the stillness and peacefulness of our inner self.

This witnessing or perpetual wakefulness is the hallmark of the fifth state of consciousness. It occurs even in the other states of consciousness. For example, when we dream at night, it is often as if we were watching the dream — what some call a "lucid" dream. Because of the expansive, spacious nature of the peace, this fifth state of consciousness is sometimes called Cosmic Consciousness. Its other names are Perpetual Consciousness or Persistent Consciousness.

Eventually, as the coherent function of the brain becomes greater, the right brain functions become even more coherent with itself, and we begin to experience this integration, including the ability to perceive energy. The peace and silence start to combine with the joy, happiness and love of the right brain, giving rise to what the yogis call "bliss." Each sensation begins to have an energy that incorporates the other sense: Sounds have a "feel," colors have a "taste," and so forth. This coherency creates a merging of the functions of the right brain, such that the peace evokes joy, which evokes love, which evokes happiness. This becomes an inherent part of experience — what the yogis refer to as *Sat Chit Ananda* or Absolute bliss consciousness. Bliss, joy and love become synonymous with the experience of awareness and the experience of self. Remember there is also coherency with the left brain. So the energy of each thought is perceived, and a blissfulness is experienced with thought, and thought becomes very subtle — almost felt as an energy. In addition, the ability to perceive subtle energies, such as the aura, come to the fore. Intuition refines and becomes a very useful tool, and all thinking becomes more intuitive. With this, the psychic abilities also start to unfold. This sixth state of consciousness is called Bliss Consciousness or Divine or Glorified Consciousness.

Finally, as the coherency and integration of the various aspects of the brain, including the emotional centers such as the amygdala, the reticular activating system that is responsible for wakefulness, and the limbic system that is responsible for much of emotion, then the subtle energies and the patterns behind creation start to become apparent. The subtle energy is perceived not just around living objects but in inanimate objects as well. Eventually subtler and subtler energies are perceived until one becomes aware of the reality that pure consciousness underlies all of creation. That may sound uncanny, but this is what physicists are discovering. All of creation arises out of one underlying field of energy and intelligence, and that field is a field of consciousness. Pure consciousness underlies not just our existence but all of creation. In the final state of consciousness we begin to directly perceive and experience that the pure consciousness in us is in everything. At a certain point, instead of us experiencing the world outside of us, everything flips, and we become the pure consciousness that is everywhere. We experience our individuality within the world that we are. The person becomes a drop in the ocean of consciousness, and they identify with the ocean and find the drop within that greater ocean. At this point we reach the final state of higher consciousness called Unity Consciousness.

The Seven States of Consciousness

State	State Name	Inner Awareness	External Awareness	Hallmark
1	Deep Sleep	None	None	Unconsciousness
2	Dream Sleep	Vague	None	Unreliable Impressions
3	Waking State	Some	Present	Ability to Interact with Environment
4	Pure Consciousness (or Transcendental Consciousness)	Fully Awake	None	Restful Alertness
5	Perpetual Consciousness (or Cosmic Consciousness)	Fully Awake	Present / Clear	Witnessing during all the states of consciousness
6	Bliss Consciousness (or Divine Consciousness)	Fully Awake	Refined Values of Objects Perceived	Subtle Perception
7	Unity Consciousness	Fully Awake	Finest Value (Transcendental Value) Perceived	"I am That; Thou art That; All this is That."

This is the level from which Patanjali speaks. He assumes his listeners know about the higher states of consciousness. He assumes they know he is describing these states. And he assumes that they know it is his love for humanity that inspires this perfect description of the possibility of life without suffering.

The First Key — The Four Quarters

We have now the first key to understanding Patanjali's gift. Almost all esoteric literature contains hidden keys that are crucial to understanding the meaning and deeper wisdom of the words. The first key to a deeper understanding of Patanjali's Yoga *Sutras* is understanding the structure of the Four Quarters that make up the collection of *Sutras*. The *Sutras* are divided into four sections that are sometimes called chapters or quarters. Patanjali gives us a map of how consciousness works by describing the different states of higher consciousness. There are four quarters — one for each of the four higher states — and each quarter is a map of that territory of higher consciousness.

Patanjali describes each of the higher states of consciousness, one per quarter, as follows:

1. ***Samadhi*** — Technically this is a state that is mistaken for enlightenment. It is the blissful state of transcendence and is sometimes translated that way. This is the state of Pure

Consciousness — it is what you experience when you transcend thought, sensation, emotion, and perception and experience pure awareness.

2. ***Sadhana*** — The word has many translations, but its root *Dha* means to set or to establish. Often implying habits or practices to establish something, this quarter is too often translated as "practice." What Patanjali makes explicit is the effects of establishing pure consciousness — the fourth state of consciousness — in daily life. He describes the development of perpetual or cosmic consciousness — the fifth state of consciousness. This quarter is more about the effects of establishing pure consciousness in daily life than instruction or guidance to getting to that state.

3. ***Vibhuti*** — In the sixth state of consciousness we become intimately aware of the energies behind creation. A blissful reverence to the beauty and glory of creation is present, such that some call the sixth state "Divine Consciousness," or what we have been referring to as Bliss Consciousness. It is also in this state that we can observe how creation creates. We experience firsthand how intention organizes consciousness and manifests changes in our daily environment. It is also in understanding this process and that subtle glory or bliss level of life that we learn to sense and work with energy and intuition. It is where the psychic abilities are cultivated and enhanced. Thus the "powers"

manifest as a result of our understanding the glory and splendor of our existence: of Being. Again, this section is a clear description of how things operate in the sixth state of consciousness. And again, Patanjali does not give us many practical techniques, but rather more a description of what this territory is about.

4. *Kaivalya*—Often translated as "isolation" or "detachment," its real meaning is this: When something is isolated, it is by itself. It is not many — it is one. This oneness is the state of Unity. It is the expression and description of Unity Consciousness. In Unity Consciousness, all is one, and there is nothing to be detached from, save our own ignorance.

These then are the Four Quarters of Patanjali:

1. *Samadhi (Transcendence - Pure Consciousness)*
2. *Sadhana (Establishing Samadhi - Perpetual/ Cosmic Consciousness)*
3. *Vibhuti (Manifestation - Bliss Consciousness)*
4. *Kaivalya (Oneness - Unity Consciousness)*

Here is another part of the key of the four quarters that can make understanding rich: Patanjali does not show us a technique or a way or a practice. In fact, Patanjali shows us a complete description of how life works. He gives us a map, but he does not tell us the details. He does not say, "In this territory you need a military jeep in order to get from here to there, and here you need to get on a boat." He does not tell us which vehicle to use to transport us through the territory — he gives us a map of how inner growth and development take place.

In his exposition of inner growth, little is offered in terms of technique or "how to." He gives the overview of the territory, so you can walk the path yourself. The wise do recognize that our growth is individual and unique. The second quarter is not about *how* to practice. It is about what shifts and changes as this higher state of *Samadhi* becomes established. Here are some of the questions he addresses:

> *Patanjali is not showing us a technique or a way or a practice. In fact, Patanjali is showing us a complete description of how life works.*

1. When we become established in silence, what happens?
2. What is the impact of that establishment on our lives?
3. What is the impact of the pure consciousness being always present?

4. What is the impact of pure consciousness being ever present in the life, especially the various areas of yoga. In other words, what is the impact of pure consciousness on the eight limbs of yoga?
5. What does meditation become as one integrates pure consciousness?

The Second Key — Meditation

Understand that for all of the development, meditation is key. For us to be fully developed and to use our full potential, we can't just wipeout the left brain; rather, our ultimate goal is to use the full potential of both right and left brain simultaneously. This full growth involves integration of both sides. But that integration will not take place as long as the dominant hemisphere, the left brain, is not given a rest. The development occurs most rapidly when we are able to allow the left brain to settle and experience more of the timelessness and peacefulness that is available in the right brain. The alteration of that experience, such as meditation with our activity, where we integrate the silence and the perception of energy, and eventually the perception and experience of bliss, into our normal functioning. There is a need for a process for us to develop these higher states of consciousness that involve the integration of the right and left hemispheres. As important as meditation is, Patanjali does not describe a technique and all of its details. In fact, at one point, he says meditate on that which

A New Paradigm

pleases. While wide open to interpretation, this alludes to the fact that he is not promoting or describing a specific technique — he is describing a state of consciousness.

This, then, is the second key to be understood. A meditation practice that is efficient and well-suited to the individual is *assumed* by Patanjali. It is difficult to understand how the higher states unfold without it.

We have already explained that in meditation we experience the quieting of the left brain as we experience the timelessness of the right brain. This is the state of pure consciousness, where we go beyond the thinking mind. Eventually this state of peacefulness and awareness is integrated with the left brain processes of thought, speech, planning, analysis, control, etc. The foundation for this, though, is the practice of meditation. Once again, it is assumed by Patanjali that we already understand and are doing this practice. Although he describes some aspects of the practice, there are few specifics, and he does not give instructions for it.

> *A meditation practice that is efficient and well-suited to the individual is assumed by Patanjali. It is difficult to understand how the higher states unfold without it.*

The Third Key — Concentration Versus Concentrated

Patanjali places loving attention on every aspect of the expressions he puts forth. The third key is to realize that this approach and attitude underlies his *Sutras*. Unfortunately, in our desire to be delivered from suffering, we too often blame the mind, human desires and emotions, as well as the feminine aspects of our own natures, and adopt a harsh attitude uncharacteristic of the loving presence of an enlightened sage. Too often we believe that we must force the mind, force the ego, and control desires.

This leads to a misunderstanding of the word "concentration." The better-fitting concept might be "concentrated." The mind naturally becomes concentrated when it is absorbed and resonates with pure consciousness. One way to understand the proper translation is to consider this analogy:

If we wanted to turn water into saltwater, then we could pour in some salt and stir. When you pour salt into water, much of it falls to the bottom of the glass naturally. If we were to measure the area right above where the salt is at the bottom, we would find it very concentrated. The concentration comes as a result of the settling of the salt. Just like the settling of the salt, concentration results from the natural settling of the mind.

A New Paradigm

What Patanjali is trying to describe is a resultant state, not a process. He is not recommending that in order to meditate we must concentrate and force the mind to be quiet (which is almost impossible to do). So it is not the process of trying to concentrate — it is the result of the mind settling. Once the mind is settled, we have the concentrated state.

The above reflects one of the major keys in understanding the *Sutras*. Too often people have mistaken Patanjali's description as the means, when in fact he is describing the end. He is describing life in transcendence, life in Pure Consciousness, life in absorption, life in awareness of the underlying field of energy and intelligence, which permeates all of life in higher states. As Patanjali has given such a brilliant analysis, we have to be careful not to mistake the description of the state for the means to get there.

> *Patanjali is describing a resultant state, not a process. He is not recommending that in order to meditate we must concentrate. Once the mind is settled, we have the concentrated state.*

We know this from our experience. It is hard to pull ourselves up from the bootstraps. It is hard to become enlightened by trying to act enlightened. It is hard to "be here now," no matter how much you try to force yourself. That is because being here now is the result of developing higher consciousness, not the means to it. It is very difficult to force yourself into a state when that state is an end-result of inner growth and development. Piaget's four-year-olds don't get to the point where they see that the cylinder of water is equal to the bowl of water by practicing the right answer. And they don't get there by trying to force themselves into thinking a particular way. They *do* end up there as a result of their internal growth. They get there by a further wiring and integration of their nervous system. The result is this ability to perceive reality accurately. That is what Patanjali describes — not a means to get there.

Yoga is not a philosophy or a religion; rather, it is a science of observation. Its principles are reproducible. Without an understanding of consciousness, the exposition gets turned into an intellectual discussion, a philosophy, rather than a description of observations that are reproducible by any human being.

The Fourth Key — The Monk Versus the Householder

Much of the esoteric knowledge of the East has come to the West via the monastic traditions of the East. Too often the tenor of yoga has taken on the influences of ascetic practices of the monastic tradition in both its interpretation and implementation. One of the keys is realizing that there is one path for monks and a very different path for householders.

A New Paradigm

The monk's path is based on loss and self-denial. The monk loses connection with his family and society, loses all his or her possessions, gives up all control over the life, and turns this over to the master. The monk undergoes ascetic practices and disciplines and loses more and more of his or herself until even the ego or "small self" is lost and only consciousness remains. There is no attachment left to any part of the small self's life. Then dawns the experience of the larger Self, the transcendental reality. The wave becomes aware of the ocean beneath it and begins to experience it throughout the life and becomes it. A state of nonattachment is achieved and eventually made permanent.

The householder's path is very different. It is not practical for the householder to give up family, society, money, and possessions in the pursuit of evolving. It simply destroys both life and the fabric of family and society to take this approach. The path of the householder is one of fulfillment. By becoming more and more fulfilled — by finding more and more fulfillment in the midst of all activity — the fullness of the Self begins to dominate the small self. The ego shrinks and becomes miniscule in comparison to the experience of the larger Self — in comparison to the experience of consciousness itself. In this way the same state of higher consciousness is achieved, and one becomes naturally non-attached.

To understand this, consider an analogy: Suppose a woman is walking down the street, and a thief steals her purse. What is the result? That depends on the inner state of the woman. If the woman is poor and homeless, the purse may represent the very last money that she has, and its loss can mean that there will be no food to eat. The suffering and stress in this situation is tremendous. The woman is very attached to the event and its impacts.

Suppose instead that the woman is a billionaire. What is the impact? The woman has so much in the bank that it just doesn't really matter. She doesn't pretend it didn't happen, but it is only a minor nuisance for her — she just goes to the bank and gets more money and new credit cards and continues on her day. She is not attached to the event. It doesn't faze her. Why? Certainly not because she decides to be unattached. It does not impact her because she *has so much*. She is so full and so secure.

When we are completely full inside — full of joy, fulfillment and bliss — then we are naturally in a state of non-attachment. This is the path of the householder. It is one of heart, of bliss, of fulfillment of desires. The heart becomes so full of love and bliss that the events of life do not overshadow one's experience of fulfillment. The householder's path is the path of bliss, and yoga plays a central role in this path. It is complete fulfillment of all material and spiritual desires through living in a state of fulfillment, joy and bliss.

A New Paradigm

This is one of the key understandings that allows yoga to be practical. It allows Patanjali's brilliance to be seen. It takes us away from a focus on the suppression of desire, non-attachment, repression of emotion, and celibacy. With a clear understanding of the different paths, we can appreciate the jewel Patanjali has given us. Students of yoga who study the Vedas will recall that there is a description of these two paths in the text known as the *Bhagavad-Gita*. In several chapters these two paths are described. In the fifth chapter, second verse, the master explains to his student:

> Both renunciation and the yoga of action,
> Lead to the supreme good, but of the two
> The yoga of action is superior to the
> Renunciation of action.

The path of the householder (the path of action) is, in fact, faster than the path of the monk (the path of renunciation). In the words of the *Bhagavad-Gita*, it is "superior." Yoga has nothing to do with suppressing desire or straining or stressing the body or with taking a religious or reverent view of life itself. Patanjali's brilliance and understanding of life far exceed that view. He offers a wisdom that transcends all paths.

Now with this background and these important keys, let us take a look at the Four Quarters of Patanjali's Yoga *Sutras*.

First Quarter

Samadhi
(Pure Consciousness)

The Process of Transcending - Key to the First Quarter

Now that we have the context for the entire work, we can begin to examine the First Quarter. To understand the essence of the first quarter, we need to have a clear comprehension of the process of transcending. We go into pure consciousness most reliably, efficiently and consistently through a process of transcending on one of the senses. The easiest sense to use is sound — the sense of hearing.

When we strike a gong and listen to the sound, the sound trails off gradually. And if we allow ourselves to pay attention and be absorbed in the sound, what we will notice is this: As the sound goes quieter and quieter, so will our mind until the sound trails off into silence. If we have allowed ourselves to be absorbed into the sound, as we hear increasingly subtle impressions of the sound, our minds will go with it into the silence effortlessly. We go beyond sound into silence. This is the process of transcending — taking a sound and experiencing quieter and quieter and quieter levels of the sound until we go into silence and are absorbed there.

When we utilize a mantra, it is not the word's meaning that is important. Thinking about the word's meaning gets us stuck in the left brain. Recall that music is processed more in the right brain. The sound aspect or sound value of the mantra is what carries us into the silence of the right brain. This is why singing the mantra is emphasized in some forms of meditation (such as Heart-based Meditation). Just saying a word or a couple of syllables over and over can keep one stuck in the left brain. It is not the word value that is important. It is the sound value that is important.

In the practice of using the sound value of a mantra, we start on the most surface level of the mind with the syllables or the memory of the syllables of the mantra. We then go more into the sound of it. As the sound gets quieter and quieter, it becomes like a notion that has a certain quality or energy — we almost feel it more than hear it. As we become more familiar with these very subtle levels, they can take on a more pleasant, and even blissful feel. This is not something we look for, because the whole process requires us to let go. This is something that happens over time.

This comes from trusting the process, from letting go, from faith and allowing ourselves to become absorbed in the pleasantness of the sound. While perceiving the energy of the sound comes frequently after many months of practice, it happens for each of us individually depending on our own sensitivity, awareness, and capacity to let go completely and to allow ourselves to just be absorbed in and enjoy the process.

Transcending is a natural process that happens effortlessly. It happens every time we fall asleep. That "falling" experience is the experience of the transcending process. We usually are not aware of it. It just happens. With meditation we are able to do this process systematically and allow ourselves to experience pure consciousness, rather than sleep.

Sound is just one sense. I have seen students learning pulse diagnosis who close their eyes and feel for more and more subtle vibrations within the pulse wave and come to a point where the pulse and everything else seems to disappear. They have transcended on the sense of touch. Sound is, however, by far, the easiest sense to use for the process of transcending.

The process, being natural, can be effortless and very efficient. Attempting to force oneself into silence is extremely hard. Transcending on sound is very easy. And transcending is key to the rapid development of higher states of consciousness.

This is what Patanajali's Yoga *Sutras* are about — the rapid development of higher states of consciousness. It is not about yoga postures. It is about the great potential we hold within ourselves for liberation and fulfillment. It is about how that part of us that is most intimate to us — our awareness and our sense of being — actually works. We can come to greater awareness starting with awareness of the body and with postures. But ultimately, it is awareness and consciousness that are most important, not the postures.

Understanding the process of transcending and going into pure consciousness is necessary to understand what Patanjali refers to in the First Quarter of his *Sutras*. It is one of the central keys.

The Second Key to the First Quarter — The Field of Consciousness

The second key to understanding Patanjali's *Sutras* is a deeper understanding of consciousness. Normally, people think of consciousness as something that takes place within themselves. Whether they see it as a result of the brain or another mechanism, they hold it to be isolated and see little connection to another person's consciousness, let alone to other living beings, let alone to the environment itself.

What physicists have discovered is that all of creation arises out of one, underlying field of energy and intelligence. Strange as it may sound, they have discovered that the consciousness of a scientist observing an experiment of quantum level events will influence the outcome of the experiment. This has resulted in many scientists asserting that the underlying field out of which everything arises is a field of consciousness itself. The is called Unified Field Theory in physics. And this just happens to be the same understanding of the ancient sages. Consciousness is not something in you. You are in it. How can we understand that?

> *Consciousness is not something in you. You are in it.*

Think of the brain as an amazing radio receiver that can tune into many stations and receive information, images and "thoughts." Although an analogy, this is probably closer to what actually happens. These thoughts are vibrating waves of consciousness. Like an ocean, consciousness can have an active set of waves on its surface, or it can be calm. Regardless of what is happening on the surface in terms of vibrations, the depth of the ocean is still. To get a sense of our individuality with this, a drawing may assist. Below we see that depending on our level of awareness, we experience ourselves as individuals (waves on the ocean of consciousness) or part of a whole ocean.

A New Paradigm

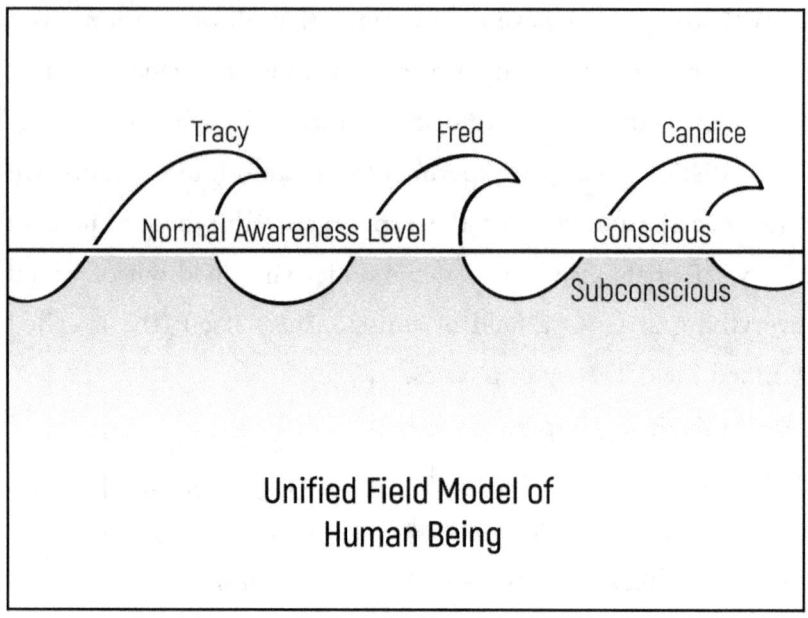

Understand that within our individual wave (our own consciousness) we can have many tiny ripples. These are the thoughts and feelings and sensations and perceptions that make up what we experience as our mind.

This understanding of consciousness as a field is important in understanding what yoga is, as defined by Patanjali. He references waves of consciousness as the stuff of the mind — thoughts, feelings, sensations, emotions, etc. This understanding of consciousness as a field that we are part of and can tap into is necessary in order to understand the first quarter.

Some other key words are also necessary. Remember: *Samadhi* is the state of Pure Consciousness when all thought and impressions in the mind cease. A Seer is one who is enlightened. Remember also: Pure consciousness is both a field and a state. When we experience only the field of consciousness, we are in the state of Pure Consciousness.

With these understandings, let us explore the First Quarter.

First Quarter - Samadhi

(Pure Consciousness)

This first section describes what yoga really is. Its focus is on the fourth state of consciousness, as that is the foundation for all the higher states of consciousness.

1. **Now yoga explained!**
2. **Yoga is the settling of the waves (vibrations) of consciousness.** *It is the settling of the mind into silent pure consciousness. Like an ocean with waves on its surface, yoga is the settling of the ocean to a completely placid state.*
3. **Then the Seer is established in the True Self.** *Then we are established in our essential nature which is Pure Being or unbounded pure consciousness. We unite with pure consciousness — Yoga means "union."*

4. **At other times, the Seer identifies with the waves of consciousness (and not consciousness itself).** *Our essential nature is usually obscured by identification with our thoughts, emotions, sensations of the body, impressions from the environment — all these are waves or disturbances in the ocean of consciousness and overshadow our awareness of who it is who is experiencing thought, emotion, etc. We think we are those things and the habits of thinking and feeling we call personality. We are not personality. We are that which is aware of and experiences personality.*

This next section tells us about what we tend to identify with (thoughts, feelings, emotions, sensations) until yoga is permanently attained.

5. **The waves (vibrations) of consciousness are of five kinds and are either creative or destructive:**
6. **They are valid knowledge, invalid knowledge, imagination, sleep and memory.** *Understanding or correct perceiving of reality, misunderstanding or misperception of reality, dreams and imaginations, sleep and memory.*
7. **Valid knowledge comes from direct experience, inference and verbal testimony.**
8. **Invalid knowledge comes from misunderstanding based on appearance that is not real.** *In other words, misunderstanding is delusion that is based on a false perception of reality.*

9. **Imagination follows verbal knowledge but without a corresponding object.** *Imagination is thought based on words and has no real physical substance.*
10. **Sleep is the wave that is based in the experience of non-existence.** *While most of us think sleep is beyond thought, sleep actually is a mental vibration that has as its impression a sense of nothingness or non-existence with which we become identified.*
11. **Memory is when the impression of an object doesn't slip away.**

This next section shows the purpose of yoga as it relates to freedom from the impressions of the mind. The focus Patanjali is giving is one of how we become free of suffering, which is based in our identification with thoughts, emotions and sensations.

12. **These five types of activity are settled through yoga and the freedom it bestows.** *These five types of internal activity or waves of consciousness (disturbances in the ocean of consciousness) are settled through yoga (union with pure consciousness).*
13. **The practice of yoga is the endeavor to become established in that state of stability.**
14. **This state becomes firmly established when cultivated (experienced) continuously without interruption.**

15. **In this state of self-mastery, one is freed from the influence of desire for objects, whether seen or heard. This is the triumph of the Self (the True Self).** *We become free of the **influence** of desire — we don't become desireless.*
16. **Through this supreme state of freedom, which comes through establishment of the True Self, one attains liberation from the world of change.**

This next section is on transcendence. This is how the process of meditation works and how coming to the state of Samadhi or Pure Consciousness occurs.

17. **This state is attained through transcending on an object** *(such as a sound)* **that takes one from gross mental activity, then subtler mental activity, then experiencing subtle bliss, to finally pure Being** *(pure I-AM-ness or pure consciousness).*
18. **When thoughts cease because of transcendence, then other impressions become dormant.**
19. **Then merging into Being, awareness of the body ceases and the mind merges with Divine Nature.** *Then thoughts merge into Being and the mind is absorbed in the infinite pure consciousness, and there is no awareness of anything external, even the body. When we transcend we go beyond sensation, and thus awareness of the body ceases.*

A New Paradigm

Understand that Patanjali was not going off on a tangent here. The reference is clearly one of the experience of being as one merges. Here are the Sanskrit words:

Bhava-pratyayah videha-prakrti-layanam
Bhava being, becoming; *pratyayah* experience (*bhava-pratyayah* experience of being, birth); *videha* one who lives at refined levels, without corporeal existence; *prakriti* nature; *layanam* merged

The progression of thought from describing transcending to merging into being is logical, and for those who have had the experience in deep meditation of merging or losing awareness of the body and being awake within themselves, this *Sutra* is readily understood. This flow of ideas continues in the next four *Sutras* as well. Here again, Patanjali does not give us specific techniques for "doing Yoga." This is also not a treatise on religious guidelines. Patanjali describes the mechanics of consciousness and its development in glorious fashion. In this section he talks about the process of transcending and going into *Samadhi*. He is giving a map of this inner territory, not a set of religious guidelines or rules. Thus, in the next verse, he is not talking about the practice of the limbs of yoga, such as *asana* or *pranayama*. He is talking about what takes place in transcending as far as the internal experience is concerned.

20. **For others, Samadhi (Pure Consciousness) is first preceded by faith, essence energy and subtle memory.** *(Samadhi is preceded by faith (or trust in letting go), by energy (the energy or feel of the sound of the mantra), and memory (the subtle notion of the mantra.) In order to transcend we have to let go of thought, emotions, and sensations. This letting go requires trust. This is the beginning of the process. As we experience more subtle levels of the mantra, we become absorbed in its energy. At the finest, most subtle level the mantra is just a notion, just the vague intention of its being there.*

The Sanskrit words of this *sutra* are as follows:

sraddha-virya-smriti-samadhi-prajna-purvaka itaresam
Sraddha faith; *virya* energy; *smriti* subtle memory; *samadhi* transcendence; *prajna* intuitive, instant knowledge; *purvaka* preceded by; *itaresam* another, whereas, in the case of others

Here we need to understand that *virya* has a deeper meaning than just energy for practicing yoga. *Virya* refers to the essential energy of something. It is used in Ayurveda to describe the essential energy of an herb, spice or food. It implies a subtle energy, not the energy of will or ego. The process of transcending requires letting go, and this incorporates, in its essence, faith. As we let go into the sound of the mantra, we come into absorption in its energy (its *virya*). As the energy takes us deeper into absorption and becomes even subtler, there is only the subtle notion of the mantra left — just its form, as it were. It is just the subtle intelligence of the form that is left. This is the *smriti* level of the mantra. *Smriti* is translated as memory, but it is really the subtle intelligence, or subtle memory, not the gross human remembering that this word refers to here.

This all leads to the next three *Sutras* that are really about this finest level of existence right near to the depths of the ocean of consciousness — right near to *Samadhi*. At this level we find great blissfulness, as we are at a very high level of consciousness.

21. **Near to it** *(to Samadhi)*, **spiritual energy** *(excitement/bliss)* **is strong.**
22. **Even in this, there is a distinction between mild, moderate and very strong energy.**

Near to *Samadhi* is intense bliss that draws us toward the infinite pure consciousness — toward *sat chit ananda* (Absolute bliss consciousness). The bliss of the mantra (its essential energy) leads or pulls us into the ocean of bliss.

23. **Or, it** *(Samadhi)* **comes from devotion** *(letting go)* **to the Divine.**

Sometimes the bliss of the energy of the mantra leads us into the silent pure consciousness. Sometimes it comes through just letting go into that field, turning the process of meditation over to something greater than our ego. This requires letting go and trusting — pure faith in the way the Universe operates.

The field of Pure Consciousness both purifies the subconscious mind, and it is also the source out of which all thought arises. It is the source of thought, creativity and intuition. It is the source of everything. It is the Universal field of consciousness.

24. **The Divine** *(experienced in its universal form as pure consciousness)* **purifies and wipes away the deep impressions that ripen into karma. It is that distinct aspect that is beyond suffering.**
25. **Therein is the seed or source of all knowledge that cannot be surpassed.**
26. **Beyond time, it is the source and the guru of all the ancient sages.**
27. **The essence of the Divine** *(the Universal Unbounded Pure Consciousness)* **is expressed in sacred sound.** *Its essence or energy is expressed through sacred mantras.*

Every sound, every form, contains within it a certain vibration of consciousness. This vibration has a quality, an essence that expresses its essential nature. On a subtle level the sound is an energetic representation of meaning. If we could take a snapshot of the process of how creation arises out of the underlying field of consciousness, we would see that at the most subtle level, the sound creates a form, and the form has a meaning. It is like when someone finds something they are looking for and says, "Ah-ha!" The sound and its energy communicate its meaning without words. At the subtle level of awareness — at the level right before entering into the silent pure consciousness — sound, form and meaning all exist together as one.

28. **Through transcending on this sacred sound, identification with pure consciousness results.**
29. **From that, one turns inward, gains pure consciousness, and obstacles cease to exist.**

This ends the section on transcending — the process of gaining *Samadhi*. Having mentioned that this state of consciousness purifies and removes obstacles, Patanjali then turns his attention to these. The obstacles that distract one from developing this fourth state of consciousness are listed here, as well as their consequences:

30. **Obstacles (*kleshas*) that distract from pure consciousness are disease, fatigue, doubt, carelessness, laziness, attachment to self-destructive habits, delusion, failure to achieve the state of Pure Consciousness and failure to maintain Pure Consciousness.**
31. **The natural results of this are suffering, unhappiness, depression, restlessness and imbalanced breathing.**

Removing the obstacles and attaining pure consciousness is central to yoga, the practice of yoga, and the application of yoga to life. The purpose of all this is to end suffering. So how do we remove them?

32. **These obstacles can be removed by repeated experience of this one reality** *(this one state of Pure Consciousness).*

This statement is key to understanding the whole next section. Patanjali has given us the solution. He has just explained the process of transcending. This is a strategy, not a technique. It is not a prescription for practice or a "how-to." It is a description of a process and the strategy of transcending as an efficient way to *Samadhi*. Now he has begun explaining what that state does to our inner experience. It removes obstacles. It cultivates friendliness and compassion. It creates changes in the breath, etc. Without understanding the key of transcending, it is too easy to interpret the following as a list of techniques to cultivate pure consciousness.

A New Paradigm

The problem with the Sanskrit *Sutra* form that Patanjali is using is that there are very few verbs. Patanjali is giving us equations where "this" equals "that." It is tempting to infer "this" caused "that" or "that" caused "this." Patanjali is reflecting the reciprocal nature of consciousness. The following eight Sutras are usually translated as prescriptions for the cultivation of consciousness and *Samadhi* — that these result from such things as compassion, equanimity, etc. Yet, just as important is the understanding that *Samadhi* cultivates compassion and equanimity.

> *Patanjali is not saying that being friendly toward the happy and compassionate toward the unhappy purifies consciousness in order to get to Samadhi. This is the error of mistaking the end for the means.*

The flow of the discourse seems to favor the later translation. Logically, we have seen that Patanjali has talked about the process of transcending removing obstacles and is now beginning to talk about the effects it has on life. It only makes sense that he would continue elucidating the effects of cultivating pure consciousness on life and on inner experience. It seems likely that the implied order may have been mistakenly altered over the centuries.

Most likely it is not that Patanjali is saying that being friendly toward the happy and compassionate toward the unhappy cultivates and purifies human consciousness so that we can get to Samadhi. This would be the error of mistaking the end for the means. The order most likely intended by Patanjali was that the cultivation and purification of consciousness creates friendliness toward the happy, compassion toward the unhappy, delight in the virtuous, and equanimity toward the unvirtuous. Putting the *Sutras* in this order allows the following *Sutras* to make sense. They are verified easily in deep states of meditation and they follow the logical flow of the discourse.

33. **Friendliness toward the happy, compassion toward the unhappy, delight in the virtuous, and equanimity toward the unvirtuous result from the cultivation and purification of consciousness.**
34. **Or** *(cultivation and purification of consciousness results)* **in the exhalation becoming restrained and the breath suspending.**

This is a common experience in deep meditation. Often beginning meditators are taken aback and feel like they cannot catch their breath. This is because in the state of pure consciousness the exhalation becomes very shallow, and the breath does suspend. We are not usually used to this, so when we come out of pure consciousness and find ourselves not breathing, we sometimes feel like we have to catch our breath. After we become used to this experience, then there is no concern or feeling of being out of breath. Suspension of the breath becomes natural in meditation.

35. **Or steadiness of mind with the cognition of refined perception.** *Refined perception is the ability to see subtle energy.*
36. **Or experiencing the brilliant light of the Self which cuts away sorrow.** *The light of the Self is often experienced as a bright white light.*
37. **Or attuning the mind to objects without desire.** *When pure consciousness is better established we are able to look at objects innocently without attraction or aversion.*
38. **Or maintaining pure consciousness during dreaming and sleep.** *This is one of the results of cultivating pure consciousness — we begin to maintain the experience in all other states of consciousness.*
39. **Or in meditation according to one's desire** *(at will).*
40. **Mastery of this** *(purification of consciousness)* **brings dominion over the supremely small to the infinitely large.**

Here Patanjali summarizes the thread from *Sutra 33* to *Sutra 40*. The effects of cultivating and purifying consciousness through the experience of the state of *Samadhi* are the removal of obstacles and the various experiences that culminate in mastery.

In this state of mastery, then, all obstacles are removed, and we attain to freedom in the state of bliss consciousness. We are to know this state of Pure Consciousness (*Samadhi*) and understand how it comes about.

Now Patanjali summarizes the entire first quarter. Again, understanding the process of transcendence is important. Allowing ourselves to get absorbed in the mantra so that it carries us further and further inward (toward higher and higher frequencies of consciousness) is important. Hence, the process of transcending starts with a discussion of absorption. A memory has energy if we are identified with it. As we purify out the stress of the emotional reaction to the trigger, the energy is dissipated, and only the impression or memory of the trigger remains — it is devoid of energy. The same is true for any stress that is being purified during the practice of meditation. As we experience finer and finer and subtler and subtler expressions of the mantra we are naturally carried into higher and higher frequencies of consciousness until we reach the infinite frequency of consciousness — pure consciousness (the Absolute).

41. **When mental activity decreases** *(in meditation)*, **then knower, knowing and known become absorbed one into another like a transparent crystal which assumes the appearance of that upon which it rests. This is absorption.**

42. In the first stage of the process the mind is mixed — alternating between the word *(mantra)*, the sound and the meaning.

43. In the second stage of the process, memories are purified of their energies and do not bind the True Self, and thus only the gross impression remains.

44. In the third stage *(feeling)* and fourth stages *(knowing)* of the process of transcending the object *(the mantra)* becomes increasingly subtle.

> *This is most important of all four quarters because it forms the basis for the others. The state of Pure Consciousness is the foundation for all the higher states of consciousness that are elucidated in the remaining quarters.*

45. The ever-increasing subtlety of objects culminates in the Unmanifest.

46. That is also the origin of Pure Consciousness.

47. In the clear experience of Pure Consciousness *(Samadhi)* dawns the spiritual light of the True Self.

48. Therein lies the level of consciousness that knows only the truth.

This is not an intellectual pursuit. It is beyond mere experience. It results in a fundamental shift in the functioning of the brain that allows it to attain a higher state of consciousness. This fourth state of consciousness purifies out the energies and stresses that remain in the subconscious mind and results in infinite freedom and unbounded awareness.

49. **The knowledge gained from direct experience of this state is different from knowledge that comes from reasoning or the testimony of others.**
50. **The impression rising from that state prevents the rising of future latent impressions of the subconscious mind** *(samskaras).*
51. **In the settledness of that state, all is calmed, and what remains is unbounded wakefulness.**

This is the end of the first quarter and the most important of all four because it forms the basis for the other quarters. The state of Pure Consciousness is the foundation for all the higher states of consciousness that are elucidated in the remaining quarters. It is the essence of yoga explained. The rest is simply further elucidation.

Second Quarter

Sadhana
(Establishing Perpetual Consciousness / Cosmic Consciousness)

The Key to the Second Quarter — The End and the Means

Another common misunderstanding has to do with mistaking an end state for the path to that state. (This was alluded to already in the First Quarter.) The yoga master who is enlightened is the epitome of nonviolence and non-attachment. The student sees this and thinks this is the means: "If only I can act nonviolently and have loving compassion for all beings and be unattached to things, then I can make progress on my path." This illusion is sometimes compounded by those enlightened or near-enlightened individuals who do not remember clearly what it is to be unenlightened.

For the enlightened or near-enlightened, it is easy to remain unattached or to have loving compassion. But that is the result of their enlightenment. It is an analogous situation to "being in the moment." When a stressful event occurs, the enlightened person will return to the peace and quiet of consciousness within them, and the event will dissipate. They stay in the moment, and any stressful feelings dissolve. They don't get attached to the event or

A New Paradigm

to the past memories and events that the situation might evoke. Thus, they don't suffer. So when their student is suffering, the teacher, having forgotten how it is to be unenlightened, reminds the student to just "be in the moment." Both teacher and student mistake this result of enlightenment — "being in the moment" — for the *means* to enlightenment.

In this manner the subject of non-attachment becomes a common confusion. The enlightened are non-attached *because* of the state they have achieved, not because they have been "trying" to be non-attached or practicing non-attachment. It happens spontaneously for them. It is the *result* of their inner state.

> *So when their student is suffering, the teacher, having forgotten how it is to be unenlightened, reminds the student to just "be in the moment."*

We are attached until we are enlightened. To "try" to be non-attached is like playing the role of the president of the United States in hopes that if we do it well enough, we will someday become president.

Even the understanding of yoga postures is fraught with this error. The ability to hold a posture with comfort for long stretches of time comes as a result of the development of consciousness, of awareness, and of freeing the body and its flows of blockages and stress, as we will see in later chapters.

Non-attachment, being "in-the-moment," being imperturbable, having infinite flexibility ("going with the flow"), possessing infinite compassion — these are all the result of progress toward enlightenment, moving toward the development of Union. These represent the end result of progress. When the means are not clear, and the student is not at the level of the teacher, then all sorts of distortions in knowledge and technique occur. Life is turned upside down, and the end gets mistaken for the means.

Patanjali is ultimately painting the landscape of each of these states of consciousness. He is involved in giving us a description of the end. He is not providing the means, the methods or the techniques. When misinterpreted as the method, then Patanjali's "Eight Limbs of Yoga" gets interpreted as steps to yoga. The freeing aspect of this understanding of Patanjali is that we don't have to focus on small outcomes. We simply attend to developing consciousness, and the rest will come.

The First Quarter dealt with the state of Pure Consciousness, which is the direct experience of being of wakeful without thoughts or sensory input — the experience of being of awake and aware without any input from the environment or the mind. There are many names for this state. It is sometimes called the Absolute, the Transcendent, Pure Awareness or Pure Consciousness, the True Self or the Self. In yogic terminology it is *Samadhi*. It stands in contrast to the familiar states of consciousness: waking, dreaming and deep sleep.

A New Paradigm

The Second Quarter deals with the effects of making pure consciousness perpetual. It discusses the effects on various aspects of the life as we move to the fifth state of consciousness. This is where the expansive holistic perception of the right brain is perpetually present, and where we experience pure consciousness entering fully into waking, dreaming and deep sleep. This can sound paradoxical: to have wakefulness and yet be sleeping or dreaming. Yet, it is something the human nervous system is capable of.

Porpoises, which actually have more gray matter than we do, need to keep swimming or they will drown. And yet, they have to sleep. They solve this dilemma by sleeping one half of the brain at a time. So half of the brain is sleeping while the other half is active and awake and swimming. Similarly, the human nervous system is capable of utilizing both hemispheres of the brain and maintaining two states of consciousness at the same time. This is what happens in cosmic consciousness where one is living silence and the experience of being (or pure consciousness) along with all activity. We have the sense of watching things unfold, of witnessing, as if we were just watching a movie.

Psychologists such as Abraham Maslow have detailed these "peak experiences" in highly functioning people. These are glimpses of higher states of consciousness.

We can have glimpses of this state of cosmic consciousness, and certainly psychologists such as Abraham Maslow have detailed these "peak experiences" in highly functioning people. While other psychologists of his time were studying dysfunction, Maslow studied normal function and ways to expand it. As part of this, he studied peak experiences of athletes and highly successful individuals. What they described to him was a sense of being in the flow, of what today many recognize as "being in the zone."

> *An example is a football player seeing a ball being passed to him and all of a sudden being in silence, watching as if time had slowed down. In slow motion he was able to completely and effortlessly perform his most amazing touchdown, reaching the pinnacle of his performance. During this time he had a sense of being totally in the flow and at the same time feeling that there was an infinite amount of time to get to the ball. A total connection to the ball was felt so there was no chance of dropping it once it was caught. For him, doing something that looked from the outside to be almost impossible and totally amazing seemed perfectly natural.*

These peak experiences occur when the integration of both hemispheres of the brain takes place. Just as the process of experiencing the fourth state of consciousness or Pure Consciousness is a back-and-forth process, so too is establishing that throughout our day. We can have these experiences of higher consciousness on and off until they get fully established — until there is no activity that is too intense or too overwhelming to take us out of the witness value.

The Second Quarter will talk about establishing (*Sadhana*) this higher state of consciousness. It will focus on describing how life works or is influenced in this state. In describing the impact of cosmic consciousness, the pure consciousness, the witness value, Patanjali describes the various areas of life that are impacted. He describes the eight limbs that are involved in attaining Union. It is important to understand that one of the key points is that the eight limbs are all part of one tree that is fed by the trunk of *Samadhi*, or Pure Consciousness. That is the trunk that feeds all the different limbs of life, and he talks about these in relation to consciousness.

Second Quarter - Sadhana

(Establishing Perpetual Consciousness / Cosmic Consciousness)

1. **Purification, study of the True Self and devotion to the Divine are the actions that stabilize Union** *(enlightenment)*.
2. **They nourish the state of *Samadhi* (*Pure Consciousness*) and weaken the causes of suffering.**

Notice that the means of purification is not specified here. No practice is specified. Patanjali gives us an overarching vision of inner development, what stabilizes pure consciousness and inner growth, and what causes suffering.

3. **The causes of suffering are ignorance, ego, attachment, aversion and the will to live** *(the ego's will to survive)*.

This is profound wisdom and insight into the nature of suffering, and it allows us to understand what to do about it. We need to look at the word ignorance not in terms of accumulated knowledge, but rather in terms of ignoring our True Self through identifying with the ego and its attachment, aversion and clinging to its fear of annihilation and mortality.

4. **Ignorance is the source of the other causes of suffering, whether they are dormant, weak, suspended or active.**
5. **Ignorance is perceiving the non-eternal as eternal, the impure as pure, suffering as happiness, and the non-self as the True Self.**

When we identify with the ego we make things seem important and lasting when they are not. We become attached to getting what we want and then get afraid that we will lose it and thus suffer even with pleasure. Our "happiness" becomes the source of anxiety and frustration. We identify ourselves with the ego and not the True Self.

6. **Ego comes with apparent identification of the Seer with the process of seeing.**
7. **Attachment is the result of pleasure.**
8. **Aversion is the result of pain.** *These program the subconscious mind.*

9. **The will to live** *(the will of the ego to survive)* **appears even in the learned.**
10. **The subtle causes of suffering are destroyed by taking them back inward** *(by transcending to Pure Consciousness).*
11. **When active, these waves of consciousness are removed by meditation.** *These waves or fluctuations of the mind, these subconsciousness tendencies, are removed by the meditation process.*

The causes of suffering are removed by the process of transcending into pure consciousness. This is the practice that establishes pure consciousness in activity. The subtle causes are also removed by taking them back to silence and letting them be purified out of the mind. This indicates a brilliant insight into mechanism by which the causes of suffering can be overcome. The explanation of this follows.

12. **Afflictions are at the root of the storehouse of past action that becomes expressed in the present or future life.**
13. **As long as the root exists, it matures into birth, life and experience.**
14. **If these are born of righteousness, then pleasure results. If born of unrighteousness, then pain results.**
15. **Change, anxiety, subconscious impressions** *(samskaras)* **cause suffering, as does opposing or resisting the activity of these** *(the activity of Nature).* **The wise recognize all of this activity as suffering.**

This is profound wisdom that is often overlooked. It is not just change and anxiety and how the subconscious mind responds to these that set up suffering. These processes are all natural results of normal activity and normal psychology. Patanjali's brilliance here is that he also recognizes a profound psychology truth — that when we resist the activity and flow of Nature, we suffer. As Jung said, "What we resist persists." In that, great suffering comes. What is the solution? Rather than getting into this predicament, it is better to prevent the resistance to Nature and prevent the subconscious programming from running when faced with change. Here is what Patanjali recommends:

16. **Avert the danger not yet come.**
17. **The cause of the danger to be averted is the identification of the Seer with the Seen.**
18. **The purpose of the Seen is experience leading to liberation. The Seen consists of qualities of the *gunas* (of Nature) — inertia (*tamas*), activity (*rajas*) and luminosity (*sattva*).**

The purpose of creation is to direct us to true happiness that comes with inner growth and leads us to true freedom. Creation is designed to lead us there. Every experience is valuable in leading there. Nothing is without purpose.

19. **The division of the gunas** *(the fundamental forces of Nature)* **extend from the extraordinary to the ordinary, from the whole of the manifest to the unmanifest.**
20. **The whole of the Seen is clear to the liberated Seer — even thoughts are witnessed.**
21. **It is only for the sake of the Seer** *(the Self and its liberation)* **that the world exists.**
22. **The identification with the Seen vanishes for the liberated Seer who has realized the purpose of all action, but it continues as the common experience of all others.**
23. **The True Self is obscured through identification with the Seen so that the reality of both Seer and Seen can be discovered.**
24. **The cause of identification is ignorance.**
25. **When ignorance is destroyed, then the Self is liberated from identification with the world. This liberation is enlightenment.**

We identify with our thoughts and emotions, our bodies and sensations, and our personality habits, and we believe that that is who we are. It is not. This is the ignorance to which Patanjali refers. As we meditate more, we begin to become aware of that part of us that experiences thoughts, emotions and sensations, and we start to identify less with the ego. We become aware that we are much more than our thoughts, habits, patterns or our personality. We come to know our awareness as separate from our thoughts.

Patanjali has summarized the process of enlightenment, so that he can discuss then the fifth state of consciousness.

26. **The means of release** *(liberation)* **is undisturbed recognition** *(discrimination)* **of the difference between the Seer and the Seen.**
27. **There are seven stages** *(states of consciousness)* **that culminate in complete wakefulness** *(enlightenment)*.
28. **The distinction between pure consciousness and the world is revealed by the light of knowledge when impurity has been destroyed by practicing yoga.**

"Practicing yoga" does not mean doing *asanas*. Patanjali's definition of yoga from the first quarter is clear. Yoga is when the mind settles, and we rest in pure consciousness. Doing this destroys the impurities that lead to the establishment of higher consciousness. It is the result of meditation, and it affects all areas of life. It creates a more integrated functioning in the brain, and a better functioning brain affects all areas of life. This is explained in the many *Sutras* that follow.

29. **The eight limbs of yoga are** *(areas of life affected by Union)*:
    a. **Yama** — The observances
    b. **Niyama** — The rules for living
    c. **Asana** — Postures
    d. **Pranayama** — Regulation of breathing
    e. **Pratyahara** — Withdrawal of the senses
    f. **Dharana** — Steady Attention
    g. **Dhyana** — Meditation
    h. **Samadhi** — Pure Consciousness
30. **The Yamas are five:**
    a. **Nonviolence**
    b. **Truthfulness**
    c. **Integrity**
    d. **Divine Conduct**
    e. **Non-grasping**
31. **These laws** *(observances)* **are universal, unaffected by time, place, birth or circumstance. Together they constitute the "Great Laws of Life."**
32. **The Niyamas are five:**
    a. **Simplicity**
    b. **Contentment**
    c. **Purification**
    d. **Study of the Self**
    e. **Surrender to the Divine**

A New Paradigm

Patanjali describes the eight limbs of yoga. Nowhere in the *Sutras* does Patanjali use the word "steps." These are the limbs of a tree, all interconnected. They operate together. The fourth state of consciousness is the topic of the first quarter of Patanjali's *Sutras*. He does not introduce the limbs until the second quarter. In his brilliance he is describing is how the limbs of life are *affected by*

> *What he is describing is how the limbs of life are affected by the fourth state of consciousness as it becomes permanent and integrated into the other states of consciousness.*

the fourth state of consciousness as it becomes permanent and integrated into the other states of consciousness. He waits until the second quarter because he is describing a map of higher consciousness and elucidating the effects of the state of Pure Consciousness (or Transcendental Consciousness) on all the limbs of the life.

Life is an integrated whole. Patanjali describes this whole, not the steps to it. It is like a table with four legs. The table is an integrated whole — when you pull one leg the entire table comes along. Patanjali describes how these areas "come along" or develop as one experiences the fourth state of consciousness repeatedly. *Samadhi* is the main limb of the tree out of which the other limbs come and from which all the other limbs are nourished. It is like moving the tabletop itself — all the legs come with it.

When we apply this to the body, the repeated experience of *Samadhi* makes the it more flexible. This is a common experience of those practicing meditation techniques that allow one to transcend. They carry less tension in the body and *asana* practice becomes easier. When *Samadhi* is experienced repeatedly over time, the breath will also tend to refine and become more efficient. One recovers from exertion faster than before. *Pranayama* or breath is affected and enhanced by *Samadhi*. Each limb is affected by the nourishment provided by the main limb. Each leg of the table is carried along as we move the tabletop.

Given this context and these keys, let us look at each of the eight limbs for a deeper understanding of the terrain that Patanjali maps out for us:

1. *Yama* — Translated as "to rein in, curb, bridle, discipline or restrain." Often these are interpreted as the "restraints." But *Yama* in the Vedic tradition represents death or the God of Death. Yama is therefore what we are dying to — what is departing from us. The result is that negative habits are "reined in." What happens specifically when the old bad habits die? Patanjali outlines these below:

    a. *Ahimsa* — Nonviolence
    b. *Satya* — Truthfulness
    c. *Asteya* — Non-stealing

A New Paradigm

  d. *Brahmacharya* — Divine Conduct (*Brahma* = The Divine Creator, *charya* = conduct or regimen)

  e. *Aparigraha* — Non-attachment (literally "non-grasping")

Each day we experience the peace and silence of *Samadhi*, we integrate this into our being, and we naturally attain to nonviolence. We have more clarity, and we recognize that lying always leads to problems in the end. We also see with this added clarity the impact our actions have on others; therefore, we do not engage in harmful actions, such as stealing or giving ourselves credit when it belongs to others or to the power of Nature.

> *Yama is therefore what we are dying to — what is departing from us.*

Our conduct becomes more divine, and, as we have more experience of the bliss value of *Samadhi*, we experience fulfillment within and are necessarily less attached. With great fullness, our happiness is within. External sources of happiness mean less and less to us. We simply become less attached. These five result from the experience of pure consciousness. They are the end, not the means.

2. *Niyama* — The prefix "ni-" negates what follows it in the Sanskrit language in the sense that it means "out" or

"away from." So the opposite of or moving away from the *yamas* or what we are "dying to" is that which we enliven or embrace. What is it that we enliven or embrace when we experience *Samadhi* or transcendence daily? Here is the list given by Patanjali:

a. *Shaucha* — purity
b. *Santosha* — contentment
c. *Tapas* — burning off of negativity ("tapasya" means heat) or purification
d. *Svadhyaya* — self-observance (observing the self)
e. *Ishvarapranidhana* — devotion to the Universal (the Divine)

Again, we see that as one practices meditation and experiences *Samadhi*, these are the results. Such a practice makes for more purity and contentment and helps us to release stress and negativity. As we start to maintain pure consciousness in our daily activity, we naturally become more self-aware, and our ability to be aware of the Self and experience the witness value of consciousness increases.

With the proper context we can understand what Patanjali described. Without it, yoga becomes religion-like — a set of "do's" and "don'ts." When we mistake the end that Patanjali is describes with the means to that end, we can create an ascetic, canonized set of rules that can actually get in the way of our personal growth and development. We cannot live the fullness of life through denying life itself. This is not inner development and not what Patanjali meant.

3. *Asanas* — The word "asana" comes from the root "sa" or "stha" which means "to establish" or "to be established." It is the same root as *Sthapatya-Veda*, the science of the natural laws of building or architecture. This word is commonly translated as "postures." Patanjali clarifies this in another *Sutra* using the word "asana" (one of three in the entire collection of *Sutras*). He states **Sthira sukham asanam**. Translated, this phrase is composed of three words: s*thira* — stability or steadiness; *sukham* — sweet or pleasant; *asanam* — established pose or postures. When one is established, then the pose is steady pleasantness or stable sweetness. How does this relate to the development of consciousness? First, to be "established" is an often-used phrase in Vedic literature that refers to maintaining higher states of consciousness — it means to be established in that higher reality or heightened state of awareness. In that state, stress and tension are gone from the nervous system and the musculature. The posture is then naturally properly aligned, as no tension or old pattern or postural habit or memory pulls it out of its natural state of alignment. In

that natural state, one is able to hold a posture without effort for long periods, up to hours, without fatigue and *with* a steady pleasantness — the sweetness of one's own bliss consciousness pervading the experience. Thus, once again, Patanjali gives us a description of the impact of higher consciousness on this "limb" of life — the result being steady pleasantness in posture or pose.

4. *Pranayama* — Again we see the word "yama." This time it references "prana" or breath. "Dying to the breath" or "the dying of the breath" is the more literal translation of this word. It is not "restraint" or "control" of the breath. Patanjali, in giving us a map of higher consciousness, alludes to the natural process that happens when we transcend — when we go into pure consciousness. In the fourth state of consciousness the breath stops, often for 20-30 seconds or more. It literally "dies." Repeated exposure to this fourth state of consciousness results in refinement of the entire human physiology. It makes the breath subtler and shallower. Less deep and forceful breathing is needed to

> *Thus, once again, Patanjali gives us a description of the impact of higher consciousness on this "limb" of life — the result being steady pleasantness in posture or pose.*

supply the body with oxygen. This again results in a "dying of the breath" that is a predictable part of the development of higher consciousness. With this refinement all sorts of techniques and use of the subtle breath become possible. Again, Patanjali describes the end, not the means.

5. *Pratyahara* — "Prati" means "away from"; "hara" means "food." This does not mean restraining oneself from the pleasures of the material world, such as food. The deeper meaning here is found in examining the word "food." The *Sutras* thus far have had nothing to do with the daily existence or daily life. They have been focused on the internal experience — on consciousness and the workings of the mind. The mind contacts the world through the five senses. It finds fascination and interest outside of itself, outside of the Self. These sensory impressions and our ideas about them "feed" the mind. The impression of the senses and the thoughts that arise as a result are the "food" of the mind. It is what feeds our interest and allows us to engage in the world. With the practice of meditation and the experience of *Samadhi*, we begin to experience the peace and then later the bliss of consciousness itself. The mind naturally "turns away" from its "food." This process of experiencing more bliss within oneself and turning within happens naturally as higher consciousness unfolds. The bliss of consciousness and the awe of being

become increasingly fascinating to the mind. It finds its "food" deep within. Attempts to "restrain" oneself from "pleasures" is trying to force the mind against itself — a process that is doomed to frustration and failure. It is confusing to the natural flow of life. It creates stress and is a hindrance to living fully in the world in higher states of consciousness.

6. *Dharana* (Steady Attention) — The origin of this word comes from the Sanskrit "dhri," or "to hold." It is most often translated as "concentration" or "holding the mind in concentration." This interpretation implies that this is a process, rather than a result. When something gains our fascination, it holds our attention. It is this unwavering attention that comes with extreme fascination, not from a habit of forcing the mind to be still. What is the most fascinating, most blissful aspect in our human existence? Pure consciousness itself is described by the ancient sages as *sat chit ananda* — *sat* meaning "Absolute" or "eternal Truth," *chit* meaning "consciousness," and *ananda* meaning "bliss." When the peace and silence of the settled mind that is attained in *Samadhi* begins to deepen, the bliss value of consciousness begins to unfold. (The acceleration of this is the subject of the Third Quarter.) It is intensely blissful and can hold the mind in great fascination. When this begins to be carried over into our normal waking

state of consciousness, the results are twofold. First, the ability to attend to things and find fascination in things grows. From an outsider's viewpoint, we appear to have greater powers of concentration. Second, the bliss of consciousness begins to be held simultaneously with all activity and all states of mind. It is like a white noise that is always in the background. Patanjali implies nothing here about the means to enlightenment. He describes the effect of the experience of *Samadhi* on the aspect of attention and its resultant ability to be effortlessly held. Great misunderstanding has filtered into the field of yoga practice regarding this particular limb. The insistence that concentration is the way to meditate and a necessary component of meditation is wholly misunderstood as it applies to the path of the householder. Concentration is the result of the settling of the mind, not the means to it.

7. *Dhyana* — Often translated as "to think" or "to meditate." Thought in higher states of consciousness naturally leads one back to the transcendent. It is like a feather that falls off a bird. It naturally winds its way back to the ground. Meditation for the householder is that process that will naturally lead the mind to the fourth state of consciousness, to the silence of pure consciousness. It occurs in a natural settling manner. As one begins to infuse pure consciousness with the waking state, then

the bliss of pure consciousness becomes more and more present. Thinking holds less fascination and will tend to trail back to silence and to pure bliss. Patanjali describes that state of higher consciousness in which meditation is a natural component of moment-to-moment existence. He describes how thought and meditation are infused with a different quality in the higher states of consciousness. Nothing in his *Sutras* implies effort, concentration, or forcing of the mind.

8. *Samadhi* — From the root "sam" meaning "together" or "integrated" and the root "dha," which is similar to "dhri" meaning "to hold," *Samadhi* is that integrated state of consciousness where the union of mind and the underlying field of consciousness occurs. The two are "held together," and in that state, thought and sensation are transcended. It is the connection with the field of consciousness that creates the nourishment of all the other limbs. Why? Because pure consciousness is that field out of which all life and all liveliness arises. It enlivens every aspect of health and physical functioning, every aspect of cognition and mental functioning, and every aspect of the emotional life. It is the source of the sap that feeds all the other limbs. In higher states of consciousness, it is a living reality. Before we attain that state, it is an experience that we

have for moments at a time until it is finally permanently integrated into all of the other states of consciousness — waking, dreaming and sleeping.

Having described the limbs of yoga, Patanjali elucidates further:

33. **For removing negativity, cultivate the opposite.**
34. **Negative feelings, such as violence, are damaging to life, whether we act upon them ourselves, or cause or condone others to do so. They are born of desire, anger or delusion. Whether mild, moderate or intense, their fruit is endless ignorance and suffering. Contemplate** *(realize)* **the opposite.**

These two *Sutras* can be misunderstood as a technique for dealing with negativity piece by piece. What Patanjali is leading to is a master solution that deals with everything through cultivating that state of awareness in which no negativity can arise. He uses the word *bhavana,* which often is translated as "cultivate," but here implies actual realization or awakening to the opposite. We realize the opposite of negativity when we integrate pure consciousness into all our functioning. The field of pure consciousness is a field of infinite positivity. When we become established in that, all negativity falls away.

Here again, Patanjali describes what happens when pure consciousness is established, not how to establish it. He uses the word *Pratisthayam*, which is composed of *prati* (to) and *sthaya* (earth/stability/being established). He describes the state of Perpetual Consciousness or Cosmic Consciousness and its effects on the *Yamas* and the *Niyamas*.

35. **In being established in** *(the state of)* **nonviolence all hostility is renounced in your presence.**
36. **In being established in** *(the state of)* **truthfulness, actions quickly yield their fruits.**
37. **In being established in** *(the state of)* **non-covetousness, all precious treasure presents itself.**
38. **In being established in** *(the state of)* **sublimation** *(of desire)*, **vitality is obtained.**
39. **In being established in** *(the state of)* **non-possessiveness, knowledge comes regarding the questions of existence.**
40. **From establishing purity** *(pure consciousness)*, **one's body is protected and preserved from** *(energetic)* **contamination by others.**
41. **Also come clarity of intellect, cheerfulness, one-pointedness, mastery over the senses and capability for knowing the True Self.**
42. **From establishing contentment, supreme happiness is obtained.**

Patanjali has given the effects on pure consciousness and its integration on the life in terms of the *Yamas* and the *Niyamas*. Now he summarizes and repeats the same concepts as at the beginning of the Second Quarter: 1) Purification, 2) Study of the Self, and 3) Devotion to the Divine. He says that through these, *Samadhi* or Pure Consciousness is made permanent.

43. **From the elimination of impurities through purification there is perfection of the body and senses.**
44. **From study of the Self, there is communion with the celestial radiant energies** *(celestial beings)*.
45. **From devotion to the Divine, Pure Consciousness (*Samadhi*) is perfected** *(made permanent)*.

Now he speaks of the effects of "being established" on *Asana* and *Pranayama, Dharana,* and *Pratyahara*.

46. ***Asana* becomes steady pleasantness.**
47. **By attaining the Infinite, the relaxation of effort and the perfection of *Asana* ensues.**
48. **With that comes freedom from duality.**
49. **In that** *(attaining the Infinite or Samadhi)* **comes the suspension of the inhalation and exhalation** *(pranayama)*.
50. **As the modifications of outer and inner breathing still, the volume becomes unobservable, the duration becomes long and the frequency becomes rare.**

51. **In the fourth state of consciousness, the entire range of inner and outer breathing is abandoned.**
52. **Thereupon the obstruction of illumination is destroyed.**
53. **And the mind becomes capable of Steady Attention (*Dharana*).**
54. **From withdrawal (*Pratyahara*), the senses cease to be united** *(identified)* **with the objective world and draw into the True Self.**
55. **From that, mastery of withdrawal (*Pratyahara*) of the senses is attained.**

What is the role of yoga *asana* then? How does the practice fit in here? What is its purpose? In the process of moving toward enlightenment, the body has to be able to hold and withstand the high energy and high frequencies of consciousness associated with higher states of consciousness. In practical terms, many of the subconscious patterns and latent impressions are anchored in the energetic body. Yoga *asana* helps us to clear the cellular memories, the impressions that have gone deep into the subconscious mind and are imprinted energetically on the physical body.

> *Yoga asana helps us to clear the cellular memories, the impressions that have gone deep into the subconscious mind and are imprinted energetically on the physical body.*

A New Paradigm

Yoga *asana* in this sense is important preparation for meditation. As has been pointed out, the ability to transcend and to integrate consciousness into our daily experience of life is paramount to inner growth and development. The key to the most rapid development is when the energetic system is cleared of emotions, impressions, programming and complexes that are held in the posture, the musculature and in the energetic body. These can be cleared with an approach to yoga that is oriented toward the chakra system, the removal of energetic blocks, and the process of purification. Yoga *asana* purifies the energetic and emotional bodies, as well as the physical body. This paves the way for a smooth and direct path to transcendence. Through that transcendence, the development of higher consciousness is greatly aided. Approaches to yoga that incorporate subtle energy awareness, such as Healing Light Yoga, Kundalini Yoga and others can be highly effective in this regard.

Patanjali said that three keys are necessary to the path: 1) Purification, 2) Study of the Self, and 3) Devotion to the Divine. Yoga *asana* practice is part of the first key to evolution. It is central to purifying the energetic and emotional bodies. It is not exercise. And it is of little value without meditation. It is preparation for meditation, and meditation is the most important practice in terms of attaining the goal of yoga — union.

Pranayama or breathing techniques are aids to yoga *asana* practice and to meditation. *Asana*, *pranayama*, and meditation were always meant to be one practice. *Asanas* are not just an exercise routine; breathing techniques are not a form of meditation. What is key is a transcending type of meditation. That is the foundation of yoga practice.

Yoga can be a powerful accelerator of the evolution process if practiced from the perspective of awareness of the energetic body. It is an important adjunct, but it is not the main part of yoga. That is why Patanjali has so few references and so little discussion about the physical body. This is a treatise on the development of consciousness and not on the practice of *asana*. Meditation is the main method. *Asana* and *pranayama* are key supporting practices.

Third Quarter

Vibhuti
(Bliss Consciousness)

Key One to the Third Quarter — Love and Bliss

This third quarter is about the development of Bliss consciousness. This state is sometimes called God Consciousness because it gives a reverence for all of creation. This is where the understanding of the high state of consciousness of Patanjali is particularly important. Remember from this highest state of consciousness, the experience of the nature of the flow of pure consciousness and the nature of Divinity is experienced perpetually. The expression of "bliss" is not just ecstasy. "Bliss" is more properly understood from the angle of love. This is where the Sufi and Christian mystics have been perhaps more explicit than the Vedic masters like Patanjali.

One experiencing the infinite unbounded pure consciousness understands its essence as the essence of the Universe, the essence of the Divine. What is that essence, as taught by the mystics of every religion and spiritual tradition? That essence is love. Bliss is an aspect of love, as is joy and gratitude. These become the background of the experience of existence for the enlightened.

In developmental terms, we can say that the incredible bliss that is experienced in meditation, after pure consciousness starts to be integrated, brings us so much love with life that we develop a reverence for all of creation and for the Creator. Hence, the term "God Consciousness." However, to simply say that we develop bliss is not accurate. We are experiencing the nature of creation *and* the nature of the universe *and* the nature of the Creator when we explore pure consciousness.

We do this exploration through the subtlest, finest feeling level of our existence. In that region right before we transcend into pure consciousness we come to know the most sublime aspects of creation (the highest frequencies of consciousness), as well as the essence of pure consciousness itself. This is what the entire Third Quarter is about: getting to know this region, the role it plays in manifestation, and the essence of pure consciousness itself.

> **We are experiencing the nature of creation and the nature of the universe and the nature of the Creator when we explore pure consciousness.**

The depth of this state of development is where Patanjali focuses. First, at this level, it is clearly known that the essence of the Divine is love. The essence of the experience of the nature of life is the bliss of love, and the natural consequence and development from that is devotion to awe of all that is — and great reverence and awe of the Creator of all that is. Remember Patanjali has described three keys to inner development: purification, study of the Self, and devotion to the Divine. We have reviewed the purification process extensively in explaining the role of yoga *asanas* in inner development. We have talked extensively about the True Self and how we come to experience this through the process of transcending. The "study," then, is coming to know this experientially in our own meditation practice. Now we must understand the role of devotion to the Divine in this process of inner development.

Devotion is too often associated with a feeling of obligation, commitment and seriousness. That is why this word is probably not ideal to convey what Patanjali refers to. When we experience something we absolutely love, then devotion is a natural byproduct. We don't have to force ourselves to attend to it — we are drawn to it naturally. If you love dancing, you become a devoted dancer — not out of obligation, not out of commitment, and not because you want to be a serious dancer, but rather because it brings such joy and bliss to your heart.

A better word than "devotion" would be "love." It is through love that the bliss value of consciousness is cultivated. Love is not an emotion. It is not a sentiment. It is beyond emotion and goes to the core of our being. It is the essence of Being. It is the essence of consciousness. It is that which pulls us into devotion and allows the fullness of consciousness to develop in the sixth state of consciousness.

The interesting thing about the development of this state of consciousness is that love and bliss cultivate the state, and the state results in love and bliss. Recalling that the right brain is where love, and happiness and peace are cultivated, it makes sense that those things that put us more in the right brain will help to cultivate more integration of those qualities and functions into daily life. Whereas the First Quarter focused on the cultivation of silence (transcendence), the Third Quarter focuses on the cultivation of bliss and love. Understand that emotions are experienced more in the limbic system and in the amygdala, whereas love is experienced more in the right brain — thus, it is not an emotion.

When we experience something we absolutely love, then devotion is a natural by-product. We don't have to force ourselves to attend to it — we are drawn to it naturally.

Love is a difficult word to work with, as it has so many romantic, sexual and other common cultural associations. In this context, it is better to express it in other terms: acceptance, gratitude, awe, joy, appreciation, reverence, faith, forgiveness, presence, caring, nurturance, trust and innocence. These all hint at this universal force that underlies all of life and that is the essence of consciousness itself — love. All of those expressions arise from our awareness and alignment with this force.

Patanjali, standing in the ocean of that essence and that force, describes the cultivation of the finest feeling level of our existence — the juncture point between the beginning of thought, feeling or desire, and the infinite, unbounded pure consciousness. The experience at this level of life is where the cultivation of the experience of bliss and the experience of the essence of consciousness originate. That is what this Third Quarter is all about.

Key Two — How Creation Manifests

In order to understand the above, as well as the descriptions that Patanjali gives to working from this level of life, we need to understand the key to this quarter — how creation manifests.

That topic is best understood by analogy. While this analogy serves, it is not too far off from what scientists and physicists are discovering about quantum physics and unified field theories. The ancient sages long ago perceived that all of creation arises out of one underlying field. Like a bubble arising from the ocean, each aspect of creation, whether thoughts, feelings, desires or physical creation itself, arise first from the underlying field. Patanjali actually says in his 13th *Sutra* that the transformation of matter is the same as the transformations of consciousness (the waves on the ocean of consciousness that we call thoughts, feelings, desires).

Like the diagram below, the level of awareness determines the level at which we perceive the vibrations in the ocean of consciousness.

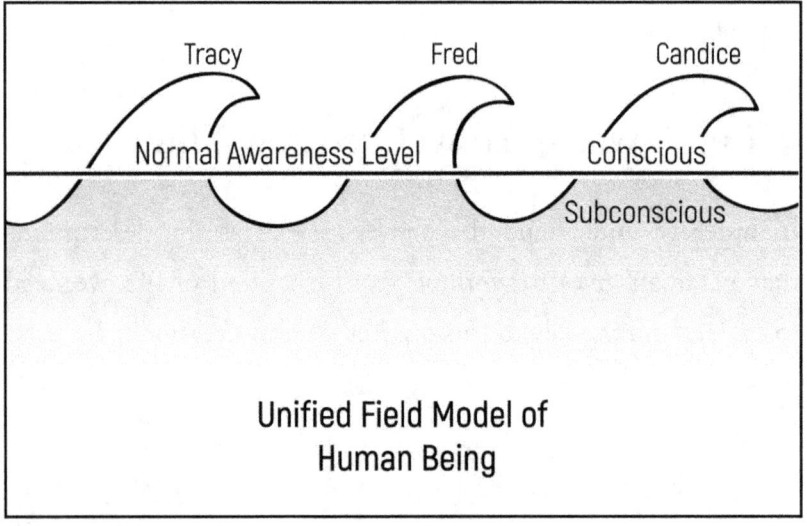

Normally we are not aware that our consciousness is part of an ocean of consciousness. Only when all vibrations or waves settle in our mind do we begin to experience the infinite unbounded nature of the ocean. Most of the time our awareness is full of vibrations or waves — our thoughts and impressions. Thus, we tend to identify with the thoughts. We also tend to experience ourselves as isolated — just as Tracy, Fred and Candice all see themselves as isolated in the above diagram.

Now imagine if Tracy could expand her awareness and drop a line down to the point of the ocean. Here she could pick up the subtle waves that Fred might be producing as they spread out and ripple through the ocean. Fred has the idea to call Tracy, and Tracy "picks up" on his vibration and calls him. Fred goes, "Wow, I was just thinking of calling you!" On this level of life, the whole of knowledge and psychic phenomena become available.

The Third Quarter talks about these abilities. It also talks about the physical transformations around matter that are possible when we master this level. These are possible because this level is not just where thoughts arise — it is also the level at which physical creation arises. It is the level where subtle laws of Nature function — where quantum mechanics operate and give us phenomena that baffle Newtonian physics.

A New Paradigm

This all being explained, the second key to this Quarter is this: These abilities are of little value in and of themselves. It is the practice of them or becoming familiar with this subtle level of life that cultivates the bliss and fulfillment that leads to higher consciousness. It is the practice that furthers the evolution. The psychic abilities may be fascinating at first, but when understood and practiced as Patanjali describes in his *samyama* process, there is no mistaking that the results are due to the Universe and not due to us or the ego. It is the mighty force of Nature that brings about the results and thus, for the yogi there is little chance of becoming attached to "doing tricks to impress friends."

More important, the result of cultivating this state of Bliss Consciousness is both fulfillment and the faith that "can move mountains." It cultivates all the aspects of love and fulfillment. It all comes from developing the finest feeling level of life and cultivating the heart. Whether one has success with every power or not is immaterial. It is the cultivation of consciousness that results and is worth the practice.

A more accurate understanding of how creation manifests comes from a model consistent with both unified field theories of physics and with the wisdom of ancient sages — the consciousness model.

ELECTROMAGNETIC SPECTRUM

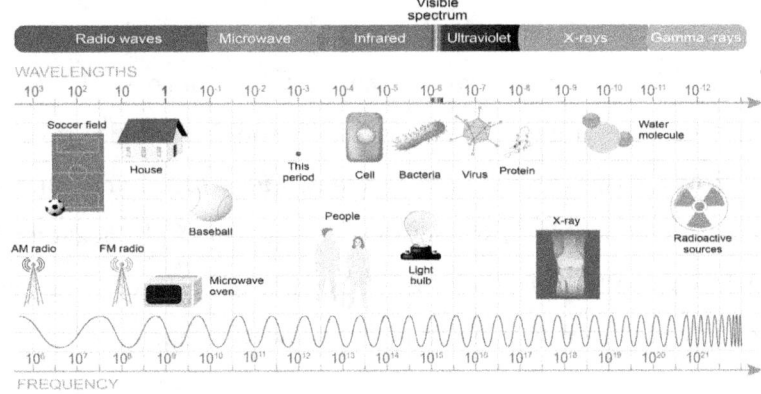

In a similar fashion, the underlying field of consciousness is also organized by frequencies. The vibrations make up the "waves" or disturbances that Patanjali discusses. The various frequencies make up the various levels of existence — mental, emotional, energetic, physical, etc. Here is a representation of the field of consciousness by frequencies:

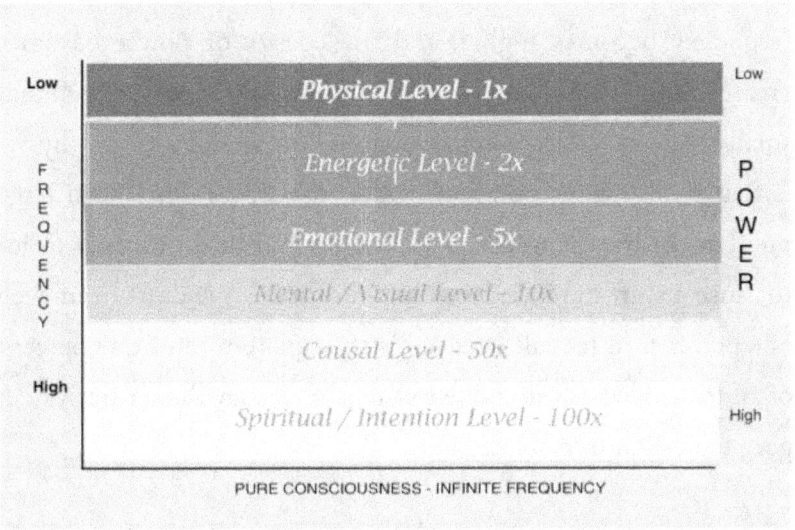

A New Paradigm

The deeper understanding here is that everything arises out of the field of pure consciousness. Consciousness is not just something that happens in our brain — our brain taps into a field of consciousness out of which *everything* arises. Every thought, emotion and desire arise out of this field. All of physical creation arises as well. (This diagram is a further refinement of the wave and ocean diagram with Tracy, Fred and Candice.)

Understand that the typical thought arises like a bubble from the bottom of the ocean. It gets larger and larger until it breaks into our awareness. All of creation arises out of this field as well. Physical creation has a very low frequency and thus seems very solid to us. Yet all matter is ultimately energy, as Einstein showed, and all energy arises out of the field of consciousness, as many unified field theories suggest.

As we draw closer to the field of pure consciousness, the frequency becomes higher, and the energy or power becomes greater. Also, the amount of coherency becomes greater, such that small shifts cause large repercussions. An analogy from physics is that with a transition from water to ice, we don't need large numbers of water molecules to line up and begin turning to ice to cause a shift in phase from liquid to solid. We don't need even one percent. In fact all we need is the square root of one percent of all the molecules, and due to their coherency the entire system goes from liquid to solid.

Similarly, near pure consciousness — right at the level before reaching it — there is great coherency, and subtle effects here can create profound changes on the physical level of life. At the finest feeling level, a subtle intention brings about a major shift. Some of these seem impossible — like they are defying the laws of nature. They are not. They are accessing the laws of nature that exist at this level of life.

The development of the sixth state of consciousness comes from experience at this level. That is the reason Patanjali talks about the intricacies of this region. He describes the settling of all vibrations into pure consciousness. Then he describes identifying with its infinite expanse and back again to a limited awareness. And he describes the technique by which intention is used to create effects from this subtle level.

When we stir three feet of water on the surface of the ocean we make little waves. When we drop the ocean floor three feet (as in an earthquake), then we create a tsunami. This is similar to the energy and effects at the bottom of the ocean of consciousness. Subtle intentions, or just the thread of an intention — what Patanjali refers to as *Sutras* — have huge, greatly magnified effects.

A New Paradigm

Cultivating awareness and the ability to operate at this level develops both the bliss of Bliss Consciousness and also the experience of Unity. With these keys in mind, let us then look at the *Sutras* of the Third Quarter.

Third Quarter - Vibhuti

(Bliss Consciousness)

1. **Dharana** *(Steady Attention)* **is attention held steady on a single point.**
2. **Dhyana** *(Meditation)* **is the flow of awareness transcending to the One.**
3. **Samadhi** *(Pure Consciousness)* **is when that object** *(the mantra)* **becomes devoid of its own nature and awareness appears by itself.**
4. **The three taken together are** *samyama.*

As is the case with the rest of the *Sutras*, Patanjali does not give us the actual technique of *samyama*. The whole work is not about technique. It describes how consciousness and the development of consciousness work. Here he gives overall strategy or process, not specific technique. The strategy involves attention, intention, and transcending into Pure Consciousness.

A New Paradigm

With attention to a specific intention, we transcend on that intention — just as transcending on a mantra — and then come to Pure Consciousness. That is the process of *samyama*.

5. **Through mastery of *samyama* the bliss of complete wakefulness dawns.**

So again, the intention is not the mastery of powers, but rather complete enlightenment.

6. **The application of *samyama* is in degrees.**
7. ***Dharana, dhyana,* and *samadhi* are internal limbs** *(of yoga)* **compared to the previous.**
8. **Even *samyama* is an external limb, though, compared to unbounded awareness** *(Pure Consciousness)*.

Now Patanjali describes the subtlest experience that occurs in the process of experiencing *samyama*. Within that we experience a transformation to stillness — a transformation to silence called *nirodha parinama*. This is the integration of pure consciousness into the mind. As this occurrence of silence in the mind happens repeatedly, it makes an impression on the mind. As one enters the pure consciousness, it goes from the one-pointed attention on the object of transcending (the intention) to the infinite, unbounded experience of pure consciousness. This is called *samadhi parinama*. This process, over time, leads to Unity Consciousness, where we experience and are aware of both the one-pointed value of consciousness and the infinite unbounded consciousness at the same time. This is called *ekagrata parinama*. This process is involved both in inner development and inner experience and also in the manifestation process that takes place with all matter. This is how Nature works. This is what the next *sutras* describe.

9. ***Nirodha parinama,* the transformation to stillness, occurs when consciousness moves toward the joyful moment of stillness, and the mind's impressions disappear, and the impressions that lead to silence appear.**
10. **The silence flows evenly into the mind, because it becomes a latent impression** *(a samskara)* **itself.**
11. ***Samadhi parinama,* the transformation to pure consciousness, is the alternation between the mind's being one-pointed and its being unbounded.**
12. **And from this comes** *ekagrata parinama*, **the transformation to Unity, the state in which activity and silence are equally balanced in the mind.**
13. **These are the transformations of the consciousness. The transformations that operate in matter — transformations of quality, form, and state — are similarly explained.**
14. **Each object carries its past, present and future qualities within it.**
15. **The diversity of matter is caused by the laws of nature, which conduct evolution.**

According to Patanjali, that is how the transformations of Nature work and how *samyama* brings about the various abilities and psychic powers. This next section expands on some of these. Note this is not a comprehensive list. While Patanjali describes how consciousness and Nature work, he is also showing how the experience of *samayama* cultivates the next state of consciousness — Unity Consciousness. This is the purpose of these practices. Many commentators have warned students not to get involved with the various psychic powers or abilities that Patanjali describes. This is unnecessary advice. In an authentic process, the student knows with absolute certainty that the effect is not of his or her making — it is an effect of Nature. No one would claim ownership of gravity and say, "Look at this trick. I just made this pen fall to the ground." Similarly, from the level of consciousness necessary to do *samyama* properly, no one can claim ownership of the resultant powers. The whole next section list various abilities that we have with this gift of a human nervous system.

16. ***Samyama* on the three transformations brings knowledge of the past and future.**
17. **Perception of an object is usually confused because its name, its form, and an idea about it are all superimposed upon one another. By doing *samyama* on the distinction between these three, we can understand the sound of all living beings.**

18. **From the direct experience of latent impressions comes knowledge of previous births.**
19. **And from the direct experience of its state, we can know the quality of another mind.**
20. **We know the quality, but not the content of the mind, because that is not within the sphere of this *samyama*.**
21. ***Samyama* on the form of the body makes it imperceptible, by breaking the contact between the eye of the observer and the light reflected by the body. From this invisibility is gained.**
22. **Karma returns both quickly and slowly. From *samyama* on that, or from premonitions, comes knowledge of death.**
23. **Through *samyama* on friendliness, etc.** *(compassion, happiness)*, **these qualities are strengthened.**
24. **The strength of an elephant, and so on, is obtained through *samyama* on these strengths.**
25. **Knowledge is gained about what is subtle, hidden or distant by allowing the inner light to come forth** *(samyama on the inner light)*.
26. **Through *samyama* on the sun comes knowledge of the universe.**
27. **Through *samyama* on the moon comes knowledge of the arrangement of the stars.**
28. **Through *samyama* on the polestar comes knowledge of the movement of the stars.**

29. **Through *samyama* on the navel plexus comes knowledge of the bodily systems.**
30. **Through *samyama* on the hollow of the throat, hunger and thirst are subdued.**
31. **Through *samyama* on the bronchial tube, calmness is gained.**
32. **Through *samyama* on the light in the head** *(the third eye or intuition)* **comes vision of perfected beings.**
33. **Through intuition everything can be known.**
34. **Through *samyama* on the heart comes knowledge of consciousness.**

In all of the great spiritual traditions the heart is emphasized. Here Patanjali makes clear that the practice of *samyama* on the heart is the key to knowing consciousness — to knowing its fabric and functioning. This is a way of experiencing the bliss and love values of consciousness and the essence of consciousness. This is the reason some meditations (such as Heart-based Meditation) place emphasis on practices that develop the heart. Through this the essence of consciousness is known.

35. **Outer experience causes identification, and the intellect is identified with the Self. Through *samyama* on the distinction between intellect and pure consciousness comes knowledge of the True Self.**

36. From that arises intuition and refined hearing, touch, sight, taste and smell.
37. These are proofs of awakening and yet are less important than *Samadhi*.
38. Through *samyama* on loosening the cause of bondage, and through perception of the movements of the mind, entering the body of another is possible.
39. Through *samyama* on the upward breath (*udana*) comes freedom from contact with water, mud, thorns and the ability to rise up *(levitation)*.
40. Through *samyama* on the even breath (*samana*), radiance is gained.
41. Through *samyama* on the relationship between hearing and space, divine hearing *(clairaudience)* is gained.
42. Through *samyama* on the relationship between body and space and through absorption in the lightness of cotton fiber, movement through space *(yogic flying)* is gained.
43. Mental activity which is external to the body and unimagined is called the "great bodiless state." Though *samyama* on that, the covering over the inner light is dissolved.
44. Mastery over the elements is gained through *samyama* on the gross form, essence, subtle form, connectedness and purposefulness of an object.

45. **From that arises the ability to become minute and so on. Perfection of the body and indestructibility of its characteristics result.**
46. **Perfection of the body consists of beauty, grace, strength and the firmness of a diamond.**
47. **Mastery over the senses is gained through *samyama* on their ability to perceive, their essence, individuality, connectedness and purposefulness.**
48. **From that comes movement as swift as the mind, existence without a physical structure, and mastery over Nature.**
49. **Solely from perception of the distinction between intellect and pure consciousness comes all-knowingness and supremacy over all that exists.**
50. **Through non-attachment even to that — through the collapsing of the seed of the *doshas*** (*that which gives rise to the fundamental elements in creation*) **— there is liberation (enlightenment).**

This is the point of this Quarter: Through the practice of *samyama* and through getting to know this finest level of life, we come to the highest state of consciousness — we come to enlightenment. At this level of life, there is full awareness of all levels of creation. The full experience and ability to perceive at the highest level of the spiritual planes becomes available. Here the perception and interaction with celestial beings even becomes possible. However, at this level of consciousness no pride or ego comes into play. There is nothing to attach one to the experience, nor is there any sense of pride. Again, at this level of life, all occurs through the forces of Nature and natural evolution. It is not done by us. It happens effortlessly and organically through the subtle laws of Nature. And as we come to know ourselves as the entire universe, it is no longer curious or special to have contact with celestial beings.

51. **There is no cause for attachment or pride in contact with celestial beings, because nothing desirable occurs.**
52. **By *samyama* on the apparent succession of moments of eternity comes the ability to discriminate.**
53. **Then comes the ability to discriminate between objects that seem similar.**
54. **Knowledge born of the finest discrimination takes us to the farthest shore. It is intuitive, omniscient and beyond all divisions of space and time.**
55. **When the intellect becomes as pure as the Self, enlightenment dawns.**

The "intellect" refers to that ability to discriminate between this or that — to notice a distinction. When the ability to notice the distinction between Self (pure consciousness) and the world at the finest level of creation is not clouded by the ego or past associations or stresses or by anything, then it is said to be "pure." Then we come to know that we are both the Self and the world. This is enlightenment. And this is the subject of the final Quarter.

Fourth Quarter

Kaivalya
(Unity Consciousness)

The Key to the Fourth Quarter — Dissolving Latent Impressions

Each of the higher states of consciousness represent more enlightened, more awake states. Some would call Unity Consciousness "full enlightenment." However, each of these states represent its own form of enlightenment, and the reality is that growth does not stop — ever. That is the nature of the universe. In Unity Consciousness we finally experience, perceive, and know the reality of creation completely. It is full enlightenment in that sense.

This is our natural state of being. This is what we were designed for. Patanjali talks about the change from one state of being (or state of consciousness) to the other as being the result of the grace or the bounty (fullness) of Nature as it unfolds our potential for maintaining higher states. We unfold in a natural way. While practicing the *Siddhis* and developing Bliss Consciousness is a profound way of cultivating the sixth state of consciousness, the final state is brought about in its own time through the grace of the Divine.

The timing of this is not up to the ego or a result of any technique, effort or self-will. It comes in its own time through the great blessings of the Universe. It comes through the free flow of grace into the life — aided when all blocks to its flow have been removed.

The key to understanding the Fourth Quarter is to understand spiritual psychology. It is to understand the process of unwinding the associations, programming and complexes of the subconscious mind, such that no subconscious programming exists. All *Samskaras* are dissolved. The subconscious is made conscious in the process of enlightenment, and the innocent mind is lived. The individual mind is like a computer in many ways, full of programming and associations. Through the process of meditation, the programming and associations are removed. The memory remains, but there is no action or reaction to remembered events; nor is there reaction to present events, because the program no longer exists.

This is why Patanjali says in the seventh *Sutra* of this Quarter that the actions on the mind of an enlightened being are neither light nor dark. They have no association. It is not that memory is erased; rather, it carries no emotional charge or inherent meaning. It is seen innocently. It is the innocence of pure presence. As the biblical saying goes, "Unless ye become like children, you cannot enter into the kingdom of heaven." The mind is so full of peace and bliss that it is not affected by the impressions and situations it takes in. They are met with full awareness and perfect innocence.

When the subconscious becomes conscious, then all patterns become conscious. This means that we are then capable of choosing to continue to run them or to discard them. We are free. The process is one of meditation and integration of the awareness gained in meditation. Soon the light and love stirring in pure consciousness replaces all the latent impressions in the subconscious mind. This is the basis for liberation and fulfillment. This is the focus of the Fourth Quarter.

Fourth Quarter - Kaivalya

(Unity Consciousness)

1. **The psychic abilities** *(the powers or Siddhis)* **may already be present at birth, or they can be developed through herbs, mantras, purification or by** *Samadhi.*
2. **Any change into a new state of being is the result of the fullness** *(grace)* **of Nature unfolding inherent potential.**
3. **The apparent causes of a change do not in fact bring it about. They merely remove obstacles to the flow and growth of Nature** *(evolution)*, **just like a farmer does to the soil.**
4. **All minds are created by ego.**
5. **The One Consciousness** *(the Divine)* **is the cause of the many minds.**
6. **And of these, only the mind born of meditation is free from latent impressions** *(Samskaras or subconscious programming).*

This points to the importance of meditation in the process of developing higher consciousness. It also point to the key to spiritual psychology. We all have associations, complexes and programming that exist in the subconscious mind.

7. **The impact of the actions on the mind of an enlightened being are neither light nor dark. Those of other unenlightened beings is threefold** *(of the three Gunas, leaving deep impressions)*.
8. **From their actions are sown the seeds of mental tendencies that bear fruit appropriate to their nature.**
9. **Memory and latent impressions** *(subconscious patterns)* **have similar forms. They give birth to our tendencies, even if separated by time, place, or lifetimes.**
10. **And these impressions are eternal as is the nature of desire.**

This is an important point as it relates to asceticism and desire. The common misconception is that we have to get rid of desire; however, if we get rid of desire, we get rid of life. Desire is not the enemy. It is the binding influence of desire, or the attachment to desire, that creates the problems and the suffering. It is being overshadowed by the desire. It is identifying with the desire. Life is not possible without desire, and attempts to suppress it will ultimately fail. Enlightenment is a state of fullness, not emptiness. In that state the mind is so full of the bliss and love — so full of light and illumination — and the heart so content — full of peace, love and bliss — that desires and their fulfillment make no impression. They have no significance. There is no attachment.

This relates to the previous example of the stolen purse. There is no attachment and no stress for someone who is a billionaire. It is this fullness of heart and the illumination of the mind that makes the state of enlightenment free from the binding influence of desire.

> *Enlightenment is a state of fullness, not emptiness.*

11. **Ignorance, fruits, the objects of desire are bound together. When the cause is no longer attached to the fruits, the effects** *(the karma)* **will no longer exist.**
12. **Throughout the past and future the Absolute Self always exists. Regardless of the path, the invincible force of evolution upholds life.**
13. **All paths, whether clear or subtle, are part of the nature of the evolution.**
14. **The true nature of reality is one of unity or evolution driving transformation.**
15. **Since minds are diverse, the paths to knowledge are different.**

16. But the reality of an object or path is not dependent on the mind to perceive it, for if it were what would become of it, if not perceived?
17. Objects are known or not known depending on whether they influence the mind.
18. But the mind itself is always known because it is witnessed by the unchanging Self.
19. The mind does not shine by its own light, as it is illuminated by the Self.
20. Not being self-luminous, the mind cannot be aware of an object and aware of itself at the same time.
21. Nor is the mind illumined by another more subtle mind, for that would imply the absurdity of an infinite series of minds, and the resulting confusion of memories.
22. Consciousness, though unmoving, gains knowledge of its own intelligence by assuming its form. *(The form of the mind.)*
23. The mind that is colored by both its object and the Self is all-comprehending.
24. And the mind, despite its countless separative tendencies, desires and impressions, exists for the sake of the Self, because it acts in association with it.
25. For the Seer who has cognized this distinction *(between the Self and the mind)*, reflection on the nature of the Self ceases.
26. Then the mind is inclined toward unity, and liberation dawns.

27. **If there are gaps in that, then other thoughts arise due to latent impressions** *(samskaras)*.
28. **The removal of these is by the same means as the removal of the afflictions.**

The last latent impressions are removed by the same process of meditation and the integration of the pure consciousness into the mind.

29. **One who has attained complete discrimination between the subtlest level of mind and the Self has no higher knowledge to acquire and has nothing to gain in the deepest absorption. They attain to the Divine and live in a state of unclouded Truth.**
30. **From that comes the removal of all afflictions and the binding influence of action.**
31. **Then all obstructions are lifted, knowledge becomes infinite, and what remains to be known is insignificant.**
32. **Then evolution has fulfilled its purpose, and the sequence of transformations is complete.**
33. **The sequence of time, which depends upon moments, ceases at the final end of the transformation.**
34. **In the absence of activity of Nature, its purpose fulfilled, what remains is liberation, the infinite power of consciousness established in its own nature. This is Unity Consciousness** *(enlightenment)*.

Making It Practical

The Last Key

Making It Practical

Esoteric knowledge is fascinating, but any wisdom that is profound must also be made practical. In order to make Patanjali's wisdom practical, we need to realize that the foundation of yoga, as well as the foundation of inner growth and development is consciousness. It is meditation that allows us to develop consciousness. Meditation is key to the process. And an effortless, mantra-based meditation that allows for transcendence is one of the best approaches. The first step in making this knowledge practical is to adopt an effortless, mantra-based meditation practice, such as Heart-based Meditation (www.HeartBasedMeditation.com). Without this, the whole foundation of Patanjali's teaching is lost. With it, his words become real and have a profound impact on the quality of one's life.

The second key is the acceleration of the process of integrating pure consciousness into our daily life. This is done by opening the body's energies to higher frequencies of consciousness through the practice of an energy-based yoga, such as Healing Light Yoga (www.HealingLightYoga.com).

The third key, and equally important is spiritual mentoring or what some call Ayurvedic Spiritual Counseling. (See newworldayurveda.com). This accelerates the process greatly through developing the skills to align with Being more directly and by releasing the ego patterns efficiently and gracefully.

The fourth key is devotion and following your heart. The bliss of the heart cultivates higher consciousness. The cultivation of pure love is what hastens evolution the fastest. It quickens the process of bringing freedom from the latent impressions. It purifies the mind and settles the heart. It brings one closer to the Divine.

To summarize, four keys are central to the most rapid inner growth and development:

1. Effortless, mantra-based meditation
2. Energy-based yoga
3. Spiritual mentoring
4. Cultivating love and following your heart

Summary

Now having fulfilled the objective of describing the four higher states of consciousness, the light of truth and the real understanding of yoga is complete. In four short Quarters and less than 200 *Sutras*, the full range of human development and evolution has been described.

The gift of knowledge and the understanding of the inner workings of consciousness is what Patanjali offers us with his *Sutras*. What a wonderful exposition of clarity and conciseness. Understanding the depth of the gift has required us to delve deeply into understanding consciousness itself. That is exactly what Patanjali intended. In knowing how consciousness unfolds, how we evolve, and the great liberation and bliss that await us is both an inspiration and a traveler's guide to the inner journey. This is a journey that will unfold for all of us eventually. With this knowledge, it can be sooner rather than later.

Patanjali has not given us rules, but rather guidelines. He has not given us techniques, but rather strategies. He has not given us religion, but rather the purest spirituality — the purest understandings of the inner workings of the human being.

With this gift, we can move forward more quickly with clarity and certainty. With this gift, we can know the way forward. With this gift, we can understand all that is to come for us. And with this gift, we are finally able to know the path to enlightenment.

Going Forward

I invite you to learn an effortless, mantra-based meditation, such as Heart-based Meditation. I invite you to engage in an energetically-based yoga practice, like Healing Light Yoga. I invite you to engage in spiritual psychology, counseling and mentoring. I invite you to take this gift and make it practical by applying meditation, yoga and mentoring to your life. Develop your consciousness. It is your greatest treasure.

Now that you know the truth and the wisdom of Patanjali, all that is left is to apply it and come to that great fullness, freedom, bliss and love. It is what you deserve.

Be blessed!

Resources

Meditation:
www.heartbasedmeditation.com

Healing Light Yoga:
www.healinglightyoga.com

Paul Dugliss, M.D.:
www.drdugliss.com
www.pauldugliss.com
www.newworldayurveda.com

www.ingramcontent.com/pod-product-compliance
Lightning Source LLC
Chambersburg PA
CBHW070614010526
44118CB00012B/1508